THE CHURCH AND THE LAND

To Mr. Andrew Nuar, with sincere thanks
for time, effort, and support contributed to IHS Press.

The Church
and
the Land

by

Fr. Vincent McNabb, O.P.

Norfolk, VA
2003

The Church and the Land was first published in 1925 in London by Burns, Oates, & Washbourne, Ltd., as a collection of various articles and essays penned by Fr. Vincent McNabb during the preceding years. As noted in the original Preface, the original form of the essays has been left intact. This edition has also largely preserved the spelling, punctuation, and formatting of the orignal.

The original edition of the work bore the *Nihil Obstat* of G.H. Joyce, S.J., and the *Imprimatur* of Edm. Can. Surmont. The author's footnotes appear at the bottom of the pages where they occur. Notes added by the IHS Press editors appear at the end of the text.

ISBN: 0-9714894-6-7

Library of Congress Cataloging-in-Publication Data

McNabb, Vincent, 1868-1943.
  The church and the land / by Vincent McNabb.
    p. cm.
  ISBN 0-9714894-6-7
  1. Land tenure--Great Britain--History. 2. Land tenure--Religious aspects--Catholic Church--History. I. Title.
  HD593 .M38 2002
  261.8'5--dc21

                                                    2002013129

Printed in the United States of America.

IHS Press is the only publisher dedicated exclusively to the Social Teachings of the Catholic Church. For further information, contact:
IHS Press
222 W. 21st St., Suite F-122
Norfolk, VA 23517 USA

Table of Contents

Table of Contents
(continued)

Reflections on Fr Vincent McNabb, O.P.
by Hilaire Belloc

I t was long a commonplace that the world knew nothing of its greatest men. Now that saying was already current a life-time ago. It is
emphatically true today, and its value and meaning affect us at the
present moment more than ever they did in the past, for this is a moment
when men are only publicly known by their names, and when the real
personality for which the name stands is hidden under a mass of popular
print.

Father Vincent McNabb, the Dominican, who has just passed to
his reward, intensely illustrates all this. The greatness of his character, of
his learning, his experience, and, above all his judgment, was something
altogether separate from the world about him.

Those who knew him marvelled increasingly at every aspect of that
personality. But the most remarkable aspect of all was the character of
holiness. Everyone who met him, even superficially, discovered this.

Those of us who had the honour and the rare advantage of knowing
him intimately and well over many years find, upon looking back upon
that vast experience, something unique, over and above the learning, over
and above the application of that learning to Thomism, which is surely
the very heart of the Dominican affair.

To that testimony, which so many have the honor and privilege to
present, I can add less than nothing. We know holiness just as we know
courage or the unimportant particular of physical beauty and proportion.

When we come across that quality of holiness permeating and proceeding from the whole Dominican world, we can only be silent as before
some very rare and majestic presentation, wholly foreign to our common
experience.

It was not the learning, though it had been accumulated over so
many years, nor the particular familiarity with the master text of St.

Thomas, it was the fullness of being which, as we remember what we have lost, is on a scale that appalls and dwarfs all general appreciation.

It would have been astonishing in any man to have discovered so profound a simplicity united to so huge a spiritual experience. Finding it in this one man, experiencing it as we did, there seems little more to be said unless for the purpose of reiteration.

I can write here from intimate, personal experience. Vincent McNabb was with me walking in our garden here in Sussex (which he knew so well!) on the chief occasion of my life, a moment, like all such moments, when the soul was in the presence of death and therefore of eternity.

I do not see how this testimony can be amplified. I have known, seen and felt holiness in person. In that presence all other qualities sink away into nothingness.

I have seen holiness at its full in the very domestic paths of my life, and the memory of that experience, which is also a vision, fills me now as I write, so fills me that there is nothing more to say.

Men of this calibre are better known in their absence than in their presence. With that absence the rest of my life will, I think, be filled. There are many indeed who can add to this testimony, but I can only add to it by an astonished silence, contemplating holiness in person and all that was meant thereby.

Of this he now has complete vision while we who write of him grope and are in darkness. Under the protection of that soul and its intelligence and virtue combined, I must fall back upon silence.

Never have I seen or known anything on such a scale.

Introduction

I t is sad to remark that in preparing this introduction I found myself reading *The Church and the Land* in a tattered library edition of 1936. The book was well-worn, read by farmers, students, and monks of a different era. Heavily thumbed and creased, my edition had travelled through two college libraries, the College of St. Benedict (St. Joseph, Minnesota) and Mary College (Bismarck, North Dakota). There was no evidence of the book having been checked out in half a century. Yet I knew that my reading copy was a fortunate survival. The book in my hands had been called to Virginia from halfway across the country because the name and works of Vincent McNabb have slipped away from Catholic memory.

The neglect of *The Church and the Land* is not unique. The Saracens of Progress are quite even handed in their destruction. My personal collection of books by McNabb and his close friends, G.K. Chesterton and Hilaire Belloc, largely comes from copies tossed away by the library of the Catholic University of America, no doubt to make way for some electrifying work of modern fancy. Trustworthy guides have always been rare finds, but now the very communities that should safeguard wisdom, trade her for grubby ephemera. It was not always so.

Vincent McNabb, O.P.: A Dangerous and Holy Crank

Joseph McNabb was born at Portaferry, Ireland near Belfast on July 8, 1868.[1] He was the tenth child of eleven, born to a sea captain and a peasant mother who both exemplified the loving and capable parenthood that so often marks McNabb's social criticism. In McNabb's own family

---

[1] Apart from McNabb's own works, the chief biographical information about him still comes from the work of a fellow Domincan, Ferdinand Valentine, (*cont'd*)

he saw an image of the Holy Family of Nazareth, for him the symbol and model of true Christian social order. Though without much money, the McNabbs were not without joy and charity. McNabb's earliest memories of his family life were of his mother's love for her own children, as well as the truly poor of the parish. McNabb set out in *Eleven, Thank God!*, a defense of the family that could thaw the most rigorous heart of our childless Age.

As a young man, his father's profession called upon the family to move to England, to Newcastle-upon-Tyne. There he was touched deeply by the life and spirituality of the Dominicans who ran the local parish. At the age of seventeen he resolved to join the Order of Preachers. From 1885 to 1891 he studied in the English Dominican noviciate at Woodchester, taking the name Vincent. Shortly after being ordained a priest he was sent to Louvain for higher studies in Sacred Theology. McNabb returned to England in 1894, and would spend his life ministering to the English, sometimes taking up pastoral or administrative work at the various priories in which he resided – at Leicester and St. Dominic's in London. For the majority of his life he resided as a parish priest at St. Dominic's.

It may strike some as curious that one of the Order of St. Dominic, an urban mendicant order, would so heartily take to the land. Yet from his early days as the young prior at Hawkesyard, McNabb had farmed small plots of land. It was through farming that McNabb's spiritual life and the social teachings of the Church united. The act of farming gave him an insight into what England had lost and what Christendom might gain. The centrality of the rural life was, of course, important in any Thomistic analysis of politics and society; and in mediaeval England Dominicans were accused, at least, of stirring up the landed peasantry against the unbridled powers of their day. Nevertheless, few Dominicans have ever shouldered the plough.

McNabb held that Catholics should break entirely with the urban industrialized miasma of London and Birmingham and flee to the fields. In England, McNabb became the major proponent of the *Catholic Land Movement*, which sought to establish clusters of homesteading families in the countryside. The self-sufficient and anti-machine ethos of the move-

---

Father Vincent McNabb, O.P.: Portrait of a Great Dominican (Westminster, 1955). Much of Valentine's useful tome is a collection of letters by and to McNabb. Also of importance is the special issue of *The Chesterton Review* 22.1-2 (1996), dedicated to McNabb.

ment bears some resemblance to the Amish. McNabb's agrarian vision, however, is more reminiscent of the Benedictine tradition. Perhaps the ubiquitous influence of Newman on English Catholicism is at work?[2]

McNabb was not clamoring for separatism, but calling for integration. Today's white-washed history, so fascinated with urbanism and high technology, would have us believe that McNabb and his compatriots were nothing but obsolete cranks. Yet in four years alone, between 1926 and 1930, 14,000 men formally applied for small-holding grants with the British Ministry of Agriculture. Seventy-three percent of those involved during the first quarter of the century stayed on the land and became established farmers.[3] In the United States, there was an even greater movement in the wake of large scale disillusionment with the volatility of finance capitalism. Between 1930 and 1932 alone, some 764,000 people moved from the city to the countryside to take up life on the land.[4] McNabb, of course, was not simply concerned with economic security, important thought this was. McNabb hoped those he persuaded would find a life, like the Benedictine achievement, at harmony with nature, a life where work, worship, intellectual leisure, and family life where all of a cloth.

McNabb concerned himself with the whole of Catholic cultural restoration. His published works reflect the breadth of his concerns. His books were sometimes the fruit of long thought, such as his monographs on the poets Chaucer or Francis Thompson. Sometimes they were the handiwork of his academic lecturing and contemplative reading, such as *Meditations on St. John* or *The Doctrinal Witness of Infallibility of the Fourth Gospel*. Sometimes they were the achievement of many wise years as a priest and popular devotional speaker, such as *The Craft of Prayer* and

[2] Cf. J.H.Newman, "The Mission of St. Benedict," Historical Sketches, vol. 2 (London, New York, and Bombay, 1906), 409–410. As a Domincan novice, McNabb was devoted to Fr. Betrand Wilberforce, a great personal friend of Newman. Wilberforce, himself something of an outrageous Dominican, would regale the young McNabb with tales of Newman; see F. Valentine, *Father Vincent McNabb*, 82–83.

[3] Some 26,000 men moved from the cities to the land with the help of government subsidies. Of these nearly three-quarters remained as successful small-holding farmers; see J.P. Corrin, *G.K. Chesterton & Hilaire Belloc: The Battle Against Modernity* (Athens and London, 1981), 152.

[4] R. Borsodi, *Flight from the City: An Experiment in Creative Living on the Land* (New York, 1933), xxii.

God's Way of Mercy. Finally, they were, at times, the convictions that he came to and held from his study of Thomistic philosophy and modern economics, and what might today be called sociology. Chief among these later works are *Nazareth or Social Chaos, Old Principles and the New Order,* and *The Church and the Land.*

McNabb and Distributism: A Thumbnail Sketch

Before proceeding further with McNabb's own social, political, and economic views, it is helpful to provide a thumbnail sketch of the movement with which McNabb is most frequently associated: Distributism.

Distributism may be described as a social disposition held by those who emphasize life as lived out in a local community. Distributists see this emphasis as the best response to the modern tendency of man to be attenuated by participation in larger abstract associations. Distributists hold that there is an organic link between the person, the family, the homestead, the city, and the State. Yet Distributists view concentrated political and economic power with suspicion and seek to influence private and public initiatives in such a way as to encourage a decentralized polity and the widespread distribution of property. Distributism encourages the orderly desire for ownership (in particular, the ownership of the means of production) among individuals, free families, and independent worker co-operatives.

Distributism was shaped initially in Great Britain by Hilaire Belloc, G.K. and Cecil Chesterton, Arthur Penty, Eric Gill, and, of course, Fr. McNabb. The movement came as a response to the perceived twin evils of Communism and the unrestricted Capitalism generated by classical liberal ideology. Both of these systems emphasize the materialist dimension of man and are marked by a false faith in the continual unfolding of Progress. McNabb and Belloc vociferously pointed to the unity of Marxism and contemporary Capitalism in their materialistic leveling of man. The point has been re-emphasized recently by Pope John Paul II in his reflection on *Rerum Novarum*: "it agrees with Marxism, in the sense that it totally reduces man to the sphere of economics and the satisfaction of material needs."[5] From the beginning, two complementary traditions of European thought opposed this two-headed liberal materialism and

---

[5] *Centesimus Annus,* §19.

deeply influenced Distributist writings: Thomism, restored to prominence under Pope Leo XIII, and the anti-Whig medievalism of late eighteenth and nineteenth-century English cultural conservatives such as Cobbett, Coleridge, Ruskin, and Newman.

Distributist ideas would enter into North America chiefly through the works of the English Distributists and the growing influence of Catholic social teaching in political and economic thought. The works of Chesterton, Belloc, and McNabb had a deep and lasting influence on Catholics in America through numerous books published by the Newman, Bruce, and Sheed & Ward presses. Print works fostered personal contacts. The American Herbert Agar, as London correspondent for the Louisville *Courier-Journal* and a regular columnist for the *American Review,* became a close literary friend with Chesterton and gave public prominence to Distributism. While Distributist ideas enjoyed broadening circulation in the 1930s and early '40s, it is little surprise given that the most successful American Distributists in the early twentieth century were Catholics, such as Peter Maurin, Dorothy Day, and members of the original Catholic Worker movement; Graham Walker and the New England Distributist League; and Virgil Michel, as well as those associated with the National Catholic Rural Life Conference.

The Distributists were among the first to identify the destruction of the countryside and the erosion of the agrarian life as a wider social problem to be confronted through a posture of local self-reliance. In the cities, American Distributists were prominent in the fight to prevent unions from embracing Communism, while simultaneously safeguarding workers from the predatory conditions of industrial and urban existence. In the face of the socialist tendencies of unions and the collusion of government and big business, the urban Distributists championed smaller enterprises and the creation of worker shareholding associations.

The closest allies of the Distributists were the Southern Agrarians and their northern associates, such as Agar and Ralph Borsodi, as well as the founder of the Catholic Worker movement, Peter Maurin. Like McNabb, Maurin was deeply influenced by the writings of Pope Leo XIII, was experienced as a farmer, and was something of a preacher himself. Maurin's original vision for the Catholic Worker movement had three essential parts: (1) round table discussions where laborers and intellectuals studied Catholic social teaching together; (2) houses of hospitality – a restoration of the medieval hospice for the poor; and

(3) agrarian colleges for the education of the urban refugee to the land. Like McNabb and Ralph Borsodi, Maurin was distrustful of the alliance between government and business. In Maurin's case the connection with McNabb is direct. McNabb's writings were of the body of literature from which Maurin heavily drew. Borsodi, on the other hand, is an American secular parallel to McNabb. With McNabb he shared a desire to convince people to return to self-sufficient homesteading. Unlike McNabb, Borsodi viewed small-scale technology as a force that could assist this process.

McNabb has been described as the most influential of the English Distributists and certainly the "most unabashedly radical." He held that machinery simply tightened one's reliance on the structure of cities and industrialization and that any back-to-the-land movement that relied on machines was ultimately inconsistent with the object of self-sufficiency. In this McNabb stands quite close to Andrew Lytle's position in "The Hind Tit:"

> How is the man who is living on the land...going to defend himself against this industrial imperialism and its destructive technology? One common answer is heard: industrialize the farm; be progressive; drop old-fashioned ways and adopt scientific methods. These slogans are powerfully persuasive and should be, but are not, regarded with the most deliberate circumspection, for under the guise of strengthening the farmer in his way of life they are advising him to abandon it and become absorbed. Such admonition coming from the quarters of the enemy is encouraging to the land-owner in one sense only: it assures him that he has something left to steal. Through its philosophy of Progress it is committing a mortal sin to persuade farmers that they can grow wealthy by adopting its methods. A farm is not a place to grow wealthy; it is a place to grow corn.[6]

Yet whereas Lytle was attempting a last ditch defense of the men on the land, McNabb—holding to the same truths—was attempting to lead men back to it. Both men saw industrial technology as a menace to traditional rural life.

Together, the Distributists and the agrarians stood for local traditions, self-sufficiency, an economic life centered on the household, the stewardship of the land, and local political activism. They stood against

---

[6] *I'll Take My Stand: The South and the Agrarian Tradition* (New York, 1930; Baton Rouge and London, 1977), 204–205.

the mechanization of society, *laissez-faire* capitalism, consumerism, cultural homogenization, the destruction of rural and small town life, and the veiled socialism of the Roosevelt administration. Together the Distributists and agrarians attempted to preserve what was described as a Jeffersonian position in American political life.[7] The journal *Free America* became the flagship publication for the alliance in America; within Catholic circles, the *Social Justice Review*, *Orate*, *Fratres*, and *The Catholic Worker* regularly printed the essays of Distributists. In the British Isles, *Eye Witness*, *The New Age*, *The New Witness* and *G.K.'s Weekly* were the principal venues, with the *Tablet*, the *Dublin Review* and T.S. Eliot's *Criterion* occasionally weighing in. Whereas the Distributists anchored their thought in what they saw as a wider natural tendency for man to flourish in a local community, the Southern Agrarians worked out of a specifically regional milieu. The Southern Agrarians' quintessential but exclusive regionalism made a lasting and effective union impossible and the two remained merely allied forces achieving little public effect after the appearance of *Who Owns America?* in 1936. In recent years, the chief heir to this tradition in North America is Wendell Berry of Kentucky.

After the Second World War, enthusiasm for the Distributist and agrarian position ebbed as most conservatives formed a common front in the struggle against Communism. Exceptions to this were Richard Weaver and Russell Kirk, both of whom were well-read in the Distributist and agrarian traditions. With a growing concern for environmental issues, the decline of the Soviet Union, and greater alarm for the destructive tendencies of a resurgent *laissez-faire* capitalism, interest in Distributism began to wax anew in the last decade of the twentieth century.

The thought of Distributist thinkers can be set out according to the following canons: (1) Subsidiarity, or the understanding that the members of a primary association (e.g., the family) must structure their lives and direct their actions responsibly and that higher associations should not – without grave cause – usurp a smaller organization's ability to accomplish its task; (2) Proprietary interest, or the commitment to the widespread ownership of property and the means of production;

---

[7] The principal texts for the thought of the Southern Agrarians remain *I'll Take My Stand: The South and the Agrarian Tradition* and *Who Owns America?: A New Declaration of Independence*, ed. H. Agar and A. Tate (Boston, 1936; Wilmington, 1999).

(3) Defense of the local, or a suspicion of private or public entities that threaten (1) or (2), and a willingness to support public policy that encourages small, locally-controlled economies over the domination of large retail chains and global corporations; (4) Craftsmanship, or the confidence that local, community-based economies tend toward greater beauty, quality, and trust between the makers and the users of goods; and (5) Agrarianism, or the belief that a rural society is the best environment for safeguarding tradition, typically understood as family-centered life, self-sufficiency, anti-majoritarianism, the dignity of labor and craftsman-ship, good health, small communities, and religious vitality.

In narrating the tradition, we place Vincent McNabb among the agrarians and Distributists. McNabb, however, was long uncomfortable with such easy labels:

> You must let me withhold either approval or disapproval, because I am not a "Distributionist;" how often I have said that I am not a politician, nor am I a communist. I have no competence to say what is or is not compatible with Distributionism. The settling of that question must be left to the Distributionists.[8]

For him, his economic and social theory was not *his*, it was not *Chesterton's*, it was not *Belloc's*, it was the social teaching of St. Thomas, of the Fathers, and of Holy Scripture. Distributism was merely Faith and Morals affecting the temporal affairs of Christians, in particular, affect-ing their social, political, and economic life.

Pro Ecclesia et foco, contra mundum

One cannot over-estimate the influence the works of Pope Leo XIII, in particular *Rerum Novarum*, had upon McNabb. Considered by many a charter for Christian social order, the great encyclical was pub-lished in 1891 within a few weeks of McNabb's ordination as a Domini-can priest. *Rerum Novarum* was in third position of a trilogy of texts one should understand as most sacred to, and most cherished by, McNabb – the other two being Holy Writ and the works of St. Thomas. *Rerum Novarum* held a special place in his Domincan heart. In drafting the

---

[8] Fr. McNabb, letter to Michael Sewell (July 11, 1931), cited in Bede Bailey, "Father Vincent McNabb, Dominican," *The Chesterton Review* 22.1-2 (1996), 45–55 at 54.

document, Leo's chief advisor had been Cardinal Zigliara, a Dominican luminary. At Hawkesyard, McNabb kept a copy of the work ever nearby and required his students to commit large portions of it to memory. A portion of his favorite passage reads as follows:

> ...the ancient working-men's guilds were abolished in the last century, and no other protective organization took its place. Public institutions and laws set aside the ancient religion. Hence by degrees it has come to pass that the working men have been surrendered, isolated and helpless, to the hard-heartedness of employers and the greed of unchecked competition.[9]

It was *Rerum Novarum* and the Catholic social teaching that preceded and flowed from it that formed McNabb's social, economic and political views, not – as is so often asserted – a merely romantic medievalism or quixotic love of the land. If McNabb favored guilds and a land movement, it was because Catholic culture had cherished such things as guilds and peasant free-holdings, and it did so for a reason: *philanthropia*, a love of man in imitation of Christ. McNabb was aflame, by demeanor and vocation, to work with and for his fellow man, the materially poor, the intellectually impoverished, and the morally indigent. What better flock for a mendicant? What better preacher for such sundry paupers? The hardship of industrial life, the material conditions that assaulted faith and family, these were of interest to McNabb because they were of interest to the Church. Politics and economics were subordinated to Faith and Morals, as well as to Reason; they were not something separate; they were certainly not something to be treated as a neutral or casual matter, to be attended to as one saw fit, detached from the personal transformation that a Catholic underwent in his spiritual life. Catholic social teachings were to him the fixed stars by which he guided his thoughts and actions.

McNabb's approach to social questions was distinctively Dominican. What do we mean by this? First, he assiduously applied Thomism to the practical problems of his day. Second, he manifested the spirit, and something of the flesh, of St. Dominic in his applications; this is evident in the profound simplicity with which each subject is set before his audience. McNabb displays at all times the lucidity of the Order of Preachers, and often he seems to conjure up the style of his mediaeval forefathers.

His speaking on the subject of social and economic issues occurred chiefly in London on Sundays near Marble Arch in Hyde Park, and

---

[9] *Rerum Novarum*, §2; cf. F. Valentine, *Father McNabb*, 133.

at various meetings of the Distributist League. The Hyde Park talks occurred nearly every Sunday from 1920 to 1943. McNabb would walk the many miles from St. Dominic's Priory through neighborhoods of every class, until he reached the Park. This precious description captures the man:

> Firstly, the appearance of the man immediately attracted attention. A slight figure of about medium height, with bent shoulders, wearing a loose, well-worn Dominican habit of coarse black and white material, a khaki haversack slung over his shoulder, thick knitted white stockings, heavy-soled, black boots usually unlaced, and a battered, shapeless, soft black felt hat, the blackness turning green with age. A keen, lined, ascetic face, with old-style steel-rimmed spectacles; a smile hovering on his lips which seemed to exude friendliness and captivate his audience. He at once impressed his listeners with his personality, and with his appearance Sunday after Sunday, he became a great favorite. The crowd at the Catholic Evidence Guild platform always looked forward to his coming, and there was general disappointment if for some reason he did not arrive.
>
> As soon as he mounted the platform, he always took out his Bible from the old haversack, read out the text of the Gospel appointed for the day, closed the Book, kissed it and than began to lecture. This text he usually contrived to introduce into the subject-matter of his talk.[10]

And this picture comes from one of McNabb's greatest secular adversaries! McNabb with his home-spun habit and stout boots tramped throughout the streets of London, lecturing and disputing with the high and low of his day. His social thought, however, was chiefly forged and sharpened for his Sunday debates and frequent Distributist League appearances.

One other forum must be mentioned. McNabb was chaplain to the craftsmen surrounding Eric Gill at Ditchling. Ditchling attempted to restore and advance the mediaeval concept of the guild, a group of artisans living a common life, sharing material resources, and following a religious rule. "At Ditchling," McNabb "met Nazareth."[11] Following

---

[10] E.A. Siderman, *A Saint in Hyde Park: Memories of Father Vincent McNabb, O.P.* (Westminster, 1950), 9–10.

[11] F. Valentine, *Father McNabb*, 142.

upon the experience of ministering to, preaching to, and learning from the community at Ditchling, McNabb would set out his social and economic views in a twelve point manifesto of sorts:

1. The "flesh pots of Egypt," which must be given up, are to be left not for the milk and honey of Palestine but that "the people may go and worship God." (Exodus 5.1)

2. To cease to live in the town while continuing to live on the town may be serving Mammon rather than God; indeed may be serving Mammon under the guise of serving God.

3. The area of production should be as far as possible coterminous with the area of consumption. The utilitarians were wrong in saying "things should be produced where they can be most economically produced." *The true principle is: things should be produced where they can most economically be consumed.*

4. Farmers should farm primarily for self-support. They should sell as little and buy as little as possible.

5. "Big" farming is mass production applied to the land. Agricultural mass production is based on the Market, depends on Transport and, together with these is controlled by Finance.

6. A man's state is not measured by his wealth; but a man's wealth is measured by his state. Hence, as state is social position based on social service, it follows that a man's wealth is measured by his social service.

7. The divine right of Property means not that some men shall have all property, but that all men shall have some property.

8. The natural defense of Freedom is the Home; and the natural defense of the Home is the Homestead.

9. As Political Economy is the child of Domestic Economy, all laws that weaken the Home weaken the nation.

10. The Family, not the individual, is the unit of the nation.

11. There are only Things and Tokens. The world-wide economic crisis, if it exists, is a dearth of things, not of tokens.

12. Now a dearth of things cannot be met by the creation or redistribution of tokens. A dearth of things can be met only by a creation or redistribution of things. [12]

After Ditchling and St. Dominic's parish, the communities closest to McNabb, and certainly the most intellectually stimulating, were the

---

[12] *Francis Thompson & Other Essays* (Ditchling, 1936), 74; cf. an earlier version in *From a Friar's Cell* (New York, 1924), 117.

circle of friends surrounding Chesterton and Belloc. McNabb was particularly close to Belloc, both intellectually and spiritually. He had been a reader of Belloc's works before they even met. He found *The Servile State* one of the few sane political treatises of its day. As time went on the two friends influenced one another's writings in ways that would be hard to untangle. What is worth noting, however, is which of this irascible pair was the superior. Belloc loved McNabb, like a younger brother loves his tougher and wiser older sibling. McNabb is said to have been one of the very few men in Europe who had any influence over the mature Belloc. After the death of Belloc's wife the bond became deeper and more spiritual; McNabb would remain Belloc's confessor for the remainder of his days.

The friendship with Belloc reveals something essential to the man: his holiness. His sensitivity and power of writing sprang from spiritual wells. It was a holiness that compelled life-long devotion. During the Second World War, despite his own frail health and the exorbitant price of petrol, the ailing Belloc insisted on driving immediately to London to witness his old friend's funeral.[13] Discovered on the study wall of Belloc after his own death, were two faded photos: one of his wife Elodie and one of Vincent McNabb.

Holiness and integrity do not mark the current whims of many in our Age. And yet, if there is to be any proper application of human reason to the problems that face us, the wise, the holy, the saintly must be brought back into the halls of our imagination and deliberation. Our memories and ideas, our instincts for living out our lives must be formed by contact with the good and noble, and not simply the lifeless twitching that comes from relying on desiccated reason.

The Need for (radical) McNabbian Conversion

Yet, a reader may ask, what really is the relevance of such thought today? Even if we accept McNabb's personal holiness, has not the science of economics so advanced that we may understand and treat our social ills much more effectively than in Leo XIII's or Vincent McNabb's day? Surely, we do not have to worry about the industrialization of the workplace or the effects of factory life on the home? The foulness of a disrupted food system has passed away as have the dark satanic mills of the

---

[13] R. Speight, *The Life of Hilaire Belloc* (New York, 1970), 524.

western landscape. Food and material wealth are in abundance; classical liberalism has won the day. Surely, no one would consider Fr. McNabb's positions as either prescient for his day or appropriate to our own. As for homesteading and small crafts, these have gone the way of the draft horse, the windmill, and the iron forge.

Well, dear reader, the fact that you have kept going after that last paragraph points to at least a whisper of hesitation over whether or not all is well. Modern man, for all his climate-controlled comforts and toys, still doubts that he has it right.

Let us turn first to the work place. In McNabb's day there was a cry to improve the hideous conditions of the worker. In certain areas, victory can be claimed – though to what body or system we should grant the laurel leaves is disputed. Certainly working conditions in many western countries are improved. On the other hand, most of the (so-called) manufacturing work that McNabb challenged so squarely has moved to the Southern Hemisphere and the Far East, comfortably beyond the horizon of suburbia. Do we really think that the working conditions at any of the mills and factories that provide our clothing, tools, and raw materials are significantly different from the slums of Pittsburg, Birmingham, or Dublin a century ago?

Even in the fluorescent glow of our western cubicles, the workplace has significant problems: the 31 hour work week achieved by the middle of the twentieth century has been abandoned, any mention of it is largely erased from our popular history.

Now let us for a moment travel to a modern North American home. Homeward the happy hunter of the free West rides, usually alone, for some forty-five minutes or more in the great symbol of his liberation, the car. Though it costs him on average over $10,000 per annum to maintain his machine, and though it slays enough people each year to be classified an epidemic, life without two or three vehicles is inconceivable.

Now let us enter the modern home. The home which is nearly a thousand square feet larger than that of his grandparents. The home which his great-grandparents paid for within a decade, and which now – if he bothers staying there for more than a few years – takes a full thirty to pay for.

Now let us sit with the modern man of the West at a meal...if we sit at all. And where is the family – that is to say, where is the other person who brings in the required second income and where are the one or perhaps two children, quite possibly the fruit of the same union?

Alas, one and all are exercising their freedoms. His spouse must work in her fluorescent cubicle a little later. To reduce her stress (the sign of her economic liberation) she must, before returning home, go to the great luminous glass-block cave, off to exercise on a never-ending plastic conveyer, while watching – with two dozen other fiercely independent and liberated women – the same cable news program prophesying wars and rumors of war.

The children eat alone, but each apparently content as they are plugged into some virtual world where one may engage in such archaic activities as fighting with swords, searching for treasure, warding off dark powers from a good kingdom, speaking with imaginary creatures, and camping under a star-lit sky. We thank the heavens that digital technology has made such youthful fun not only safe, but possible.

Food, food still unites the family. That is to say, no matter where or what you eat in the United States, you and your loved ones will all be partaking in flavors created in laboratories from the same part of New Jersey. The flame-broiled low-fat burger picked up on the way back from aerobics, the country-style chicken breast prepared "just the way you like it®" in the microwave, the Thai take-out that the children wolf-down as they learn more about an endangered rainforest from the Tourism channel, all were produced along the same corridor, off the Jersey turn-pike near South Brunswick.[14]

This is, of course, a comical picture, merely a satire. Every age has its difficulties, no? At least we are secure in ours. Yet we must admit, though, that when McNabb warned that the family and the life of the family was imperiled, he was not wrong. Something as small and distant as industrial capitalism and something as near and menacing as canned food were anathema to Fr. McNabb. They were of the same beast: a dreadful beast crouching to devour the mother and child, left undefended by the father. Whether by a true choice or no, women have been swept from the home and from the life that was dignified and *their own*. And men, men have taken up the life of socio-economic nomads: knowing no allegiance to work – for work knows them not – and slowly forgetting what duty and paternal piety mean. If this is in doubt, let us turn again to our modern household.

Our Age now views as domesticated a woman who subscribes to an illustrated cooking magazine, and prepares brined beef with the precision of a German chemical engineer. Lost is the art of cooking without a refer-

---

[14] E. Schlosser, *Fast Food Nation* (New York, 2002), 120–129.

ence library. Pasta and sauce from a jar constitute a home-cooked meal. That we are momentarily satisfied with this state may be due to genuine advances in natural or organic food preparation, or it may only be a conditioned response enabling us not to face social deficiencies.

There was a time when cooking, sewing, and all the domestic arts were natural and vocational expressions of womanhood. Mothers did these things because their love for family called forth beauty and care. Now, when such things are done, they are done as a hobby to refresh the slightly guilty conscience. Guilty, because all too often the hobby is done poorly and without the object of affection: children. When asked privately working women admit they desire more children than their careers allow. The lucrative industry revolving around well-known domestic divas and cooking clubs belies our domestic (and hence political and social) happiness. Womanly arts and feminine traditions have been obliterated and only through the scrutinizing of manuals are all the crafts and treasures of women kept from utter ruin. Thankfully, there is still affection, and with affection the desire to restore the home, if only some clear path could be shown.

Man, having longer been callous, and longer disenfranchised from his own arts, seems happier than the modern woman. The pressure of being sole bread-winner is gone, a work less dreary, no? Again, we collide with our illusions. Let us harden ourselves to the probable sting that comes to most men when they contemplate that our economic system blocks them from being the economic sustainer of the family. The joint-worker household is not an exercise in freedom, but a necessity for most. The two cars (and half-ton truck), the twenty-five hundred square foot house, the clothing, the gadgets, the vacations, all require two incomes. We are surfeit with what McNabb called secondary wealth to the point that we are rarely enjoying what is primary (health, and the food and shelter necessary to our station in life). To what end are men fierce providers? Their jobs and lifestyles long insulate them from the experience of husbandry, paternal sacrifice. Their co-worker spouses are not in any real sense dependent, socially or even economically – or rather, the dependency too often becomes a kind of contractual benefit in a rabidly materialistic world. What they supply for their children, they know in their hearts, is ephemeral junk to be replaced at the next birthday or special occasion by yet more plastic and electric gadgetry.

For a small group, Do-It-Yourself shops allow some expression of craft to emerge from the eviscerated life of a white-collar worker.

One could also mention camping and certain sports as activities that still remind the male worker of his masculine flesh and sinew. Yet these activities, engaged in by an ever decreasing number of the population, are again done as hobbies or "stress-relievers," they do not constitute part of a natural cycle of life nor are they done as part of a process of enhancing and creating primary wealth. Instead, modern men drink deeply of nostalgia. They ponder catalogues that speak of "hardware" and "restoration" and buy non-mechanized toys, or at least ones using an archaic device called a "spring." With haggard determination they hunt; they hunt across the internet for old Boy Scout manuals. And when particularly adventurous (and the weather is clement) they stride boldly onto the patio and cook for their family meat (made all the more adventurous thanks to E. coli O157:H7) over an open flame (produced by something called a "clicker" and hard lava rocks that themselves have been manfully picked out at the department store). Outdoor skills have been transformed into knowing how to adjust a butane compressor properly, while holding an insulated mug, or steering a riding lawn mower – while holding an insulated mug. And yet, many still act out these exaggerated and absurd deeds from a sense of affection, weakened, it is true, by our Age and our wealth, but still there.

This domestic scene, fixed somewhere between satire and tragedy, ought not to depress us. Let it arouse us. It is something, after all, with which to make a start. Traditions may yet be restored, precisely because human nature is so enduring. At moments of crisis clarity can come forth and heroism and sacrifice be readily observed. But therein lies the difficulty. One cannot shore up the family and the community, one cannot bring dignity back to the worker or craft back to the workshop, one cannot set sail on the wild and romantic seas of monogamous marriage, by leaping from crisis to crisis –at least not willingly (normally, husband and wife do not *seek out* extreme experiences). A natural life, with sane and regular rhythms, is not the product of constant crisis –tempered by crisis, yes, but a healthy organism seeks equipoise and peace. A natural life is the product of a small, healthy community, grounded in the common, traditional, and religious life of the West.

In worship, and not in any particular economic or social scheme, lies man's end and thus his fulfillment and joy. Worship, particularly the sacramental life of the Catholic Faith, once evoked a whole way of life, a way of life evident in the peasant cultures of Europe and parts of the

Americas. That this life was filled with a spirit of sacrifice, a different ghost than that which guides the global economy now besetting us, is apparent to those who observe history. As another disciple of St. Thomas, Josef Pieper, wrote:

> Divine worship, of its very nature, creates a sphere of real wealth and superfluity, even in the midst of the direst material wants—because sacrifice is the living heart of worship. And what does sacrifice mean? It means a voluntary offering freely given. It definitely does not involve utility; it is in fact absolutely antithetic to utility. Thus the act of worship creates a store of real wealth which cannot be consumed by the workaday world. It sets up an area where calculation is thrown to the winds and goods are deliberately squandered, where usefulness is forgotten and generosity reigns. Such wastefullness is, we repeat, true wealth; the wealth of feast time.[15]
>
> A festival is essentially a phenomenon of wealth; not, to be sure, the wealth of money, but of existenstial richness.[16]

It was with such existential wealth that McNabb concerned himself. This was the wealth of Christendom, the wealth that had sprung forth from a society ordered by a clear understanding of the implications of the Mystical Body of Christ. The world of Truth, of Beauty, and of the Good was understood as a world of intermediary hierarchies radiating from Christ the King and informing each and every element worthy of existence. Public life was the fruit of the interior life and sacramental life; public life was the sterling mark of a rich and effusive love affair with the Redeemer of mankind. For McNabb, public life was natural to man and involved Nature; public life entailed a stewardship of creation. Prayer and contemplation called for a specific social order, a social order that in turn provided the common graces to dignify the common man and guide him towards eternal beatitude.

Hence the gravity of the problem perceived by McNabb. To the degree that there is not a Christian social order, the souls of men will be assailed and scorched. To the degree that there is not an honest Christian social order, the life of virtue – and indeed salvation itself – lie beyond

[15] Josef Pieper, *Leisure: The Basis of Culture*, tr. A. Dru (New York, 1963), 59.

[16] Josef Pieper, *In Tune with the World: A Theory of Festivity*, tr. R. and C. Winston (South Bend, 1999), 19.

the eye of the needle, and Man becomes a lusty camel satisfied with this world's blandishments. Man becomes a rich, well-fed, well-paid, and thoroughly amused beast.

Joy, both eternal and temporal, evades modern men and women. Why? In the name of freedom we have been told to forsake the very material conditions which might support a life befitting human dignity. Everyday becomes a day calling us to practice heroic virtue. We are conditioned to suspect as coercive, confining, or outdated institutions such as the family farm and the tradition of the family-directed business and craft; indeed, we now fear the family itself.

And yet...does anyone still grow restless like McNabb upon scanning the horizon? The answer, thankfully, is yes. There are, of course, the remnant of Western communities that never abandoned the traditional peasant life of the West: we find this remnant in the remote farms of Poland, Ireland, and Mexico. We find it in North America among the Amish and Mennonites. Nor has the West lacked thoughtful men who have seen the problem and tried to steer men away from proletarian existence: the original Catholic worker movement, the Southern Agrarians, Russell Kirk, and Wendell Berry.

What is more, the very voice that in McNabb's day tried to call men from their lotus-slumber still calls. The Catholic Church still holds that the world is in need of redemption. And for those willing to look beyond the proud prelates of the Church and the conveniently distracting scandals, much of the message is the same, if lacking in McNabb's Thomistic lucidity and Irish wit. Ironically, as the Church increases her study of globalization, She remains constant in her praise of traditional ways of life.

In contrast to the darkness that has come with Globalization, Pope John Paul II has highlighted the perennial goodness of those who farm and steward the land, those who "see God's fidelity" most directly and who, through "prolonged contact with the wonder of earth products" see the land and its fruits as "the inexhaustible gift of divine Providence." "The consequences of industrialization" as well as the haphazard development of urban areas have brought social and environmental disruption:

> If the world of the most refined technology is not reconciled with the simple language of nature in a healthy balance, human life will face ever greater risks, of which we are already seeing the first disturbing signs.... Work in such a way that you resist the temptations of a productivity and profit that are detrimental to respect for nature.[17]

Here John Paul II echoes the magnificent address given to the Italian farmers by Pope Pius XII: "We well know how much the moral recovery of the whole people depends on the steadfast faith and social integrity of the tillers of the soil." Recently, the Holy See, in fact, has outlined a policy for societies and governments to pursue, where still possible, the protection of the family, small-farm holdings, and the environment. To the surprise of those who have seen McNabb and the distributist tradition as out of step with the "advances" made by Rome on the issue of economics, the Pontifical Council for Justice and Peace has called for public and private initiatives that will curb the concentration of wealth, slow urbanization and industrialization – especially where it is at the expense of life agricultural life, curb the unjust purchasing power of urban inhabitants, introduce the concept of social mortgage (as opposed to Lockean property rights), re-emphasize the Church's teaching on the universal destination of wealth, protect the development and sustainability of family-sized farms, and promote the wider distribution of property and ownership, especially among the poor.[18]

Meanwhile, those who believe that Rome has, with the 1991 publication of *Centesimus Annus*, abandoned the Church's earlier social economic tradition and moved in the direction of classical liberalism fail to note the heavy qualifications placed on any approval of the market system. Additionally they must dismiss or ignore the subsequent criticisms of the resurgence of classical liberal economic policy.[19] And they cannot pretend that it is or was the intention of the Church, with John Paul's concessions to the "free economy" or the "market economy," to contradict Herself by retracting or softening the condemnation of economic liberalism which forms one of the essential bases of the earlier social encyclicals such as *Rerum Novarum* and *Quadragesimo Anno.*

McNabb would have been pleased with the Church's constancy, if distressed at the decline of faithful support for the social teachings – especially among lay and clerical intellectuals since his day. Not only are the worker and his rights, the life of traditional agricultural societies,

---

[17] Pope John Paul II, "Homily to Farmers from Around the World Observing their Jubilee"(November 12, 2000), §2–4.

[18] Pontifical Council for Justice and Peace, "Toward a Better Distribution of Land," promulgated in Rome on November 23, 1997.

[19] E.g., the clear condemnation of economic "neo-liberalism" in *Eccleisa in America* (1999), §56.

and the wide-spread distribution and just stewardship of resources still championed, but the life of the family remains as well at the center of the Church's discussion of a Christian social order.

If such teachings are to be more than manualistic cookbooks of Christian knowledge, they must of course be anchored to Christian tradition. There exists a tradition. But if tradition is to remain a living force, it must be handed down to those who will practice and defend the life envisioned. Vincent McNabb's work points to a concrete attempt to replace the twisted lights of a crooked Age with the lamp of perennial wisdom. Let us read McNabb and not *react*; but armed with principles, confident and humble, let us *act*. Let us put aside shadows and tokens and seek instead a life natural, dignified, and holy.

William Edmund Fahey
Christendom College
Front Royal, Virginia, USA
April 5, 2003
Feast of St. Vincent Ferrer

Preface

If a book is not merely one page of printed matter after another, but is a unity of thought and purpose made public under a manifold of words, then these garnered essays may deserve to be called a book.

In republishing them the writer has not purposed merely to make men read a book of his, but has sought to persuade men to accept a challenge and even to organize a crusade.

If he has kept the essays in their original form instead of moulding them into a logical unity, it has been under the conviction that the human lineaments they now bear may commend them to human sympathy; without which no heroic venture ever came into being or begetting.

These garnered essays are no mere craftsmanship of the library, they are not just a student's ascetic or mystic contemplations, they might almost be called the blood-spurtings forced from the mind and heart of a priest in life's fighting line, by the pressure of defence and attack. To that priest who recalls the distant years of their beginning, they are as imperative and tragic as the bugle-call "Come Home!" in the still hour before nightfall.

Some of the statistics are no longer recent or accurate. Yet they have been left untouched; if only because the intervening years, whilst slightly falsifying their arithmetic, have but verified their message or their forecast.

"For us, Catholics, the Distributive State (i.e., the State in which there are as many owners as possible) is not something which we discuss, but something we have to propagate and institute. No advance in social thought or social action is possible if we are seeking to prove to ourselves as a theory what we should be trying to realize as a fact."

A Call to Contemplatives

W E HAVE PLACED this chapter at the beginning of the book because we could not place it also at the end. Nevertheless, we wish our readers to place this chapter at the beginning and also at the end of their reading of the book. If the thoughts and hopes that have inspired it do not inspire some of our readers, the book will have been written in vain.

Indeed, not only will the writing of the book, but even the many years of life and thought behind the book, have been in vain. To find no one answering our Call to Contemplatives will seem to give the lie to one of our deepest and most matured convictions. If there is one truth more than another which life and thought have made us admit, against our prejudices and even against our will, it is that there is a little hope of saving civilization or religion except by the return of contemplatives to the land!

As in these matters of matured conviction the chronological order is often identical with the logical order, our readers will pardon what seems auto-biography, but is an effort after condensed economics and mysticism.

*****

The present writer has had opportunities for observation which few of his contemporaries even in the priesthood have equalled. Drawn from childhood by the dream of helping in the conversion of England, the Master whom he served has led him, during a life-time, into contact with almost every sphere of Catholic and social activity. It has been his privilege to know most of the foremost Catholics in the country. Many have been his friends, and his teachers. His debt towards them is insolvent bankruptcy.

Gradually, and almost in spite of his youthful convictions, it was borne in upon him that – apart from sin – the main evil in the body politic and ecclesiastic was a displaced centre of gravity. The great industrial town which had naturally fascinated his eyes of youth and dimmed his vision to the land, coming at last into focus, was seen to be not the flower and scent of social life but the scurf and putrescence of decay. Scarcely had industrialism run two hundred years than the great towns were reduced to such a state of economic bankruptcy – and here was the call to an apostle – that race suicide could be made the only practical agenda for the people.

Whilst his conviction was growing from the mere sight of a religious crisis out of an economic crisis, he was increasingly conscious of a verification of his almost unwillingly admitted conviction. For over a century there had been a concentration of ecclesiastical effort in the industrial town rather than in the country. Indeed, there had been something akin to *intense cultivation* of the town and something like under-cultivation of the country. Yet ecclesiastical statistics seemed quite decisive that, in spite of the numerous growth of people and churches, the Catholic population of the great industrial town was not keeping pace with the growth of the population. In contrast with this scanty yield for our intense cultivation of a rural industrialized people was the fact that Catholic people on the land could hardly yield anything but a dogged and devoted Catholic faith. It was not Ireland, but industrial Ireland that was Protestant; it was not France, but industrialised France that was free-thinking. If there was a crisis in the fortunes of the Church it was because the economic centre of gravity had become misplaced by a subtle avarice which was endeavouring to serve God and Mammon.

The call to fulfil our apostolic duty by telling our contemporaries these discomforting facts would have found us dismayed had not a papal command made sloth high-treason. The *Rerum Novarum*[1] of Pope Leo XIII had said: "Every minister of holy religion must bring to the struggle the full energy of his 'mind' and all his powers of endurance." And the programme demanding this energy of mind and power of endurance was outlined in these simple words: "The law therefore should favour ownership and its policy should be to induce as many as possible to become owners."

*****

Thereupon came the great lesson from Exodus; which after much disjointed thinking finally took this form. "No people has ever left the town for the land, or remained on the land when it could have gone to the town, except under the motive of religion." In other words, by a sheer exercise of economic and ethical induction we had stumbled upon the great principle of Jesus Himself, "Be not solicitous therefore, saying, What shall we eat? or, What shall we drink? or, Wherewith shall we be clothed? For after all these things do the heathens seek. For your Father knoweth that you have need of all these things.

"SEEK YE THEREFORE FIRST THE KINGDOM OF GOD AND HIS JUS-TICE, and all these things shall be added unto you."† And the principle of the Master became all the more moving because it was recorded by that disciple who had quitted the counting-house to follow Jesus of Nazareth.

*****

This divine confirmation of a truth which we had culled in medita-tion upon the widowed land of England and the crowded slums of St Pancras seemed to grow – against our will – into the conviction that all our apostolic work in which we had spent, and intended to spend, our life would be useless without some order of contemplative men going back to the land.

Gradually we seemed to think that what our apostolic thinking had concluded to be a necessity, some of those who loved Church and Moth-erland might accept as a challenge and a vision. We even went so far as to outline some of the things our apostolic thirst for truth would say to the youths who might be moved by the challenge and the vision. Here are disjointed fragments of our soul.

...SEEK...FIRST the Kingdom of God, and His justice. First things first, for God's sake; or you will crash at once. Let your Exodus be after the coming out of Egypt. Leave the garden cities and the flesh pots, not in order to scorn suburbia or to lead a simple life, but to worship God.

Quit most of your fellowmen not because you hate them or despise them, but because you love them so much as to hate the conditions which degrade and enslave them. Do not leave Babylon[2] as hating the Babylonians, but as hating Babylon, which kills the Babylonians. Leave St Pancras[3] because you love every one of those thirty thousand families living each in one or two rooms in St Pancras.

---

† St Matt. vi 31–33.

Quit Babylon for love of the Babylonians. And do not seek ease or security you can obtain by using Babylon. What will it avail you to cease living in Babylon if you do not also cease living on Babylon?

If God allows you a plot of soil, and hands for toil, why should you be solicitous to have your revenues from Babylonian brickworks – your meat from Babylonian cold-storage – your drink from Babylonian water-works – your clothes from Babylonian cloth-factories? Is there no clay in Sussex soil – are there no cattle in Sussex meadows – is there no water in Sussex wells – is there no wool on Sussex sheep? Be a *monastery* then – a MONK – a thing apart, aloof from the world; indeed, be a world apart, a self-sufficient, self-supporting kingdom; and though you surround your-selves, your lands with a high wall of brick and a higher wall of silence, your sermon will be the heart and hope of all the sermons we apostles will preach in the daily exercise of our craft of apostle.

Seek...First...His Justice

Study not merely to give God His due by worship, but to give man his due by justice. Let not individual poverty beget, as uncurbed it will beget, collective riches. What is superfluous to your poor estate *distribute*. This is distributive charity; a virtue so sacred that crimes against it are the forerunner of inevitable doom.

Measure your lands by your needs. Measure your needs not by the world's measures, but by the ell or by the King's Arm. Let your standard be not Babylon, or Thebes, or Paris, or New York, or London – but Bethlehem, Nazareth, Capharnaum, Calvary.

Go forth, Christian soul, to the unfallen earth, and there amidst the tares and briars sing the song of work that is worship. Soon around your croft will gather a sheaf of homes and homesteads, where the GREAT SACRAMENT may prepare the ploughman for the furrow, the monk for the choir, the priest for the Altar.

DIEU LE VEUT.[4]

FIAT.[5]

First Things First

A DISCUSSION in *The Times*[6] on unemployment has not been without its aspects of wisdom. Not that the contributions have always been a display of wisdom itself, but rather a stimulus to the wise. The suggestions made by the disputants have often been so frankly foolish that the wisdom of some alternative course became apparent. Thus Mr. George Lansbury[7] begins his letter with his wise saying, "We want to stop the system by which one section of the nation lives on the labour of the rest." But his letter ends with the threat, "Labour will go on with its campaign – work or maintenance, with emphasis on *work*." How a demand for more and more work will end the system of one section working for the other non-working section we are at a loss to see.

But we see that the policy advocated by Mr. George Lansbury and others will tend to perpetuate instead of destroying the system which has given rise to this evil of unemployment and under-employment, now such a national epidemic. To see this tendency we must remember that unemployment or under- employment as such is not an evil, except insofar as some kind of work is a necessary worship of the good God, and is therefore good. Nor is the modern epidemic of unemployment an evil because those who lack work lack wages, seeing that wages or token-wealth is not a good except insofar as it can obtain life's goods. Unemployment, then, is only an evil insofar as it creates for the unemployed a dearth of goods.

It is admitted that in this or that particular epidemic of unemployment the evil flowing from the epidemic may be met by providing employment and therefore wages. It is in this sense that Mr. George Lansbury looks to more "work," and therefore more wages, as the local treatment which will soothe, if not cure, the particular epidemic of unemployment now rife in London. It is in this sense that we understand the action of the authorities of Cork who have recently given citizenship to Mr. Patrick Ford because he has built a large motor factory on "the pleasant waters of the river Lee"!

But the cure of particular outbreaks of an epidemic sometimes per-
petuates the epidemic, by blinding men to the real cure. A Wage System
which is engaged in the creation not of primary wealth, but of secondary
wealth, will do nothing to cure the evil of Unemployment, insofar as it is
an evil. Labour as such should be first employed in making things of first
importance. When these primary needs are supplied, then may labour go
on to supply secondary needs,

It would be well to enumerate these primary needs if only for the
sake of realizing how far we are from finding them provided by the present Industrial System. Our primary economic necessities are: (1) Food
– i.e., bread, vegetables, milk, meat, malted liquors, etc.; (2) Clothing
– i.e., woollen, linen, and cotton stuffs, well tanned or untanned leather;
(3) Housing – i.e., a home of sufficient rooms, a homestead, fresh air, etc.
; (4) Fuel; wood, coal, etc. All other things belong to man's secondary
needs.

Now it may be startling to some men to be reminded that the present Factory System of Industrialism *produces* none of the primary needs
of human existence. The land and the land alone gives us the simplicities of Food, Clothing, Housing, Fuel. Factory methods cannot give us
these necessities of life; but they can give them a quality which makes
them controllable by a small group of men who wish to make money by
controlling them. Thus milk when doctored with boracic preparations,
or sterilised, can be controlled by a milk combine. Even fish can be so
treated by cold storage as to be always as controllable and indestructible
as wheat.

Hence when poor Mr. Lansbury (now in jail!) clamours for Work,
he wants primarily not work but a wage; and he does not seem to realize that the work he and his fellow-workers want will produce *none* of
the necessities of life. The 25,000 unemployed in his district of Poplar,[8]
if given employment, would pass into the manufacture of furniture, or
motors, or into the road or rail transport system, or some other system for
producing things of secondary need and value.

As I write this in N.W.5,[9] within a stone's throw of some of the
worst slums in the world, two trams or buses, brilliantly lighted, have
passed through these slums in one minute. Each of these has cost enough
to build almost half a dozen homes for working-men! Yet few propositions issuing from the Labour Party consider any other proposition than

that of carrying on the present bankruptcy system of neglecting our land and of producing only secondary needs. Is it more than significant that the Triple Alliance of Coal Miners, Railwaymen and Transport Workers belong to the three main secondary industries?

It will become clear that the unfortunate employees of these great (parasitic?) industries in seeking by Trade Union action to stabilize the wage basis of their service are helping on, not the riches but the poverty of their class. It should not be impossible for them to imagine the *state of things* (a significant phrase) which would result if the vast majority of workers were engaged in producing the primary needs of life. How cheap would bread be if most men were engaged in rearing wheat, and few manufacturing motors! How different or how impossible would the men be if for everyone who was engaged in manufacturing expensive furniture or luxurious clothing ten thousand were building houses! How different would this country be if few were engaged in making money and many in making things.

The only policy for Labour to adopt in order to draw the fangs of Unemployment is to put first things first. They must have the courage to discourage all attempts to engage them in luxurious or secondary production by the promise of higher or more secure wages. But if, having been challenged by this call to "first things," they follow their masters' desire to make money rather than to make things, the ghost of Unemployment will haunt the streets where they are penned – and the jails where they are imprisoned.

FORM A1

An Attempt at a Social Balance Sheet

M Y MIND HAS, of late, been turned to the subject of a social balance sheet. Only within the last year or thereabouts have I been forced to realize the social function of accountancy, which undertakes to discover amidst the chaos of modern industrial finance the soundness or unsoundness of a business undertaking.

Indeed, I have found, to my amazement, that your Scottish accountant is a professional man, habituated to examinations, who has to spend at this study of his craft twice or thrice as long as the three noble professions of the priest, the lawyer and the doctor. And he thoroughly deserves it.

And no wonder his apprenticeship lasts into mid-life. The roots and branches of the modern factory system are so many and so intergrown that judgement on the soundness or unsoundness of a business demands expert knowledge beyond the intelligence of more than a learned few. Modern accountancy is thus as intricate – and as socially useful – as modern professional billiards. Long years of study or practice go to make the skilled accountant or skilled billiard-player; and when he is made, he is hardly worth the making.

But the modern accountant has been one of the first to discover, or invent, that marvellous contrivance called the Balance-sheet. No doubt the mystics, as usual, were before the rest of the civilization by their quaint yet vital device called the Examination of Conscience. Nevertheless, I am of the opinion that the financiers and the mystics are historically and psychologically too far apart for finance to have borrowed or even stolen anything from Mysticism.

Therefore, waiving the historic point whether the Examination of Conscience is father or father-in- thought or even father-in-law to the balance-sheet, I wish to point out how even a balance-sheet in general has some good qualities rarely to be found in any balance-sheet in particular.

Thus I believe that some genius or some saint – or some compound of genius and sanctity – might draw up a "dummy balance-sheet," whereby the modern man could gauge the soundness or unsoundness of modern civilization – or, if you will, of modern civilizations. I have said "genius" and "saint," for various reasons; but for one reason in the main. Every balance-sheet, even of the soundness or unsoundness of modern civilization, must consist of certain heads of classification, e.g., Income and Expenditure, Capital, Interest – Ordinary and Extraordinary, etc.

Now to classify is to assume, to philosophize or even to dogmatize. A financier who has been bold enough to impose the classification of "Income, Expenditure," has settled, by a stroke of his typewriter (N.B. – The metaphor "by a stroke of his pen" has now only an antiquarian interest), economic disputes as subtle as the philosophic disputes about the existence of an intelligent First Cause. Moreover, as the Common-wealth is or should be chiefly concerned with the Common Wealth or the Common Good, and as that alone is good which is the true object of a good will, it follows that only a saint with his heroically goodwill must be the ultimate court of appeal about the heads of classification. (Dear reader, think this out for ten years and I believe you will see that it is true.)

The ordinary social journeymen who have beaten out their brains at a social balance-sheet have usually drawn it up with such irrelevant questions as: What is the National Income – the National Debt? How many towns of over 100,000 are there? How many adults are illiterate? Are there many noble public buildings – e.g., Houses of Parliament, Government Offices, Factories, Multiple Stores, Workhouses, Prisons, Asylums? How great is the mileage of the Railways? Are the motor-roads kept in good repair? Are the Cinemas up-to-date? Is Labour cheap and plentiful? Are school-teachers paid well? Are there fine school buildings? Is hereditary legislative power within the reach of all (i.e., who can afford it?) etc., etc.

I will not discuss this social slop-work; because if anyone cares to live under this kind of civilization he richly deserves it. But in contrast with this I will set down the outline of a balance-sheet which I will safe-guard with two preliminaries.

(1) As the family, not the individual, is the psychological unit of the Commonwealth, so the Home, not the room (or flat, or lodging), is the economic unit of the Commonwealth. For this reason amongst the many means of testing the soundness of a civilization the best means is by applying the test of Home. I have therefore called the balance-sheet Form A1.

(2) *"Bonum est ex integra causa, malum ex quocumque defectu."* A thing is good when all its parts, and not some of its parts, are good. But a thing is bad even when not all its parts but some of its parts are bad. Hence when applying the following balance-sheet we must be careful not to think that a civilization is good because it gives a satisfactory answer to one or more questions. If it gave a satisfactory answer to all the questions but one, the civilization would be evil. *Malum ex quocumque defectu.* In giving these headings I do not mean them to be exhaustive, but merely suggestive. Therefore:

In the name of the Holy and Undivided Trinity, the Maker and Model of all Social Life, let me set down some headings of a Social Balance-sheet.

(1) *How many families have a Home?*

Two pitfalls must here be shunned. The word Home commonly means an institution – e.g., "Home for mental defectives; home for dogs; John was brought up in a home."

Again, a room or two or three are not a Home. Neither are diggings a home; nor lodgings, nor a hostel, nor a hotel. If any of my readers does not know what I mean by the word Home, God pity him! He proves my thesis!

(2) *How many workers live over their work?*

This seems a dark saying, But if a man will peer into it, he will find it is a darkness heralding a dawn. A civilization based not on Home-work but on Factory-work is a civilization not resting on its base, for the Family or Home is the unit or base. Therefore – *anathema maranatha*[10] to factory civilization – i.e., Damn Birmingham, Sheffield, etc. (N.B. – *Damn* is here not a swear word, but a statement of ethical values.)

(3) *How many mothers (women?) go out to work?*

Stated in terms of industrialism, the home is the most important factory in the Commonwealth. Other factories make commodities called (often by a courtesy title) boots, hose, furniture, jam, margarine (the

Lord preserve us!), Boxo, and the whole inferno of tinned beastliness whose name is legion. The home alone makes boys and girls, men and woman, good men and good women, good Englishmen and good Englishwomen. And without these human commodities of what use are even the finest "canned goods"?

(4) *How many children are in the average family?*

Read (3) over again. You will see that this efficient factory called the Home is the more efficient the more commodities it can produce, and the better the finish it can give them. Now the best of all training in the three essential civic virtues of Poverty, Chastity, Obedience, is in the large family. *Experto credite Roberto.* Trust Bob, at his job.

(5) *How many mothers suckle their offspring?*

To appreciate this question, read 3 and 4 over again. Then read them a second time. If you don't see the point at the second reading – consult a doctor.

(6) *How many workers or shop-keepers work on Sunday?*

To work on Sunday is to work seven days in seven – and 365 days in 365 In the end it usually means hospital for three months, jail for a year, or Lunatic Asylum for life. Any Englishman who works willingly seven days in seven does not need to be threatened with hell; he has made one of his own. "The wages of sin is death."

(7) *How much concrete is used in building the average house or building?*

Concrete is fluid building material. It is of first importance in a civilization where labour has become fluid or jellified. On microscopic examination this jellifying or fluidifying of labour will be found to mean the Servile State of free men. "Which is absurd" (Euclid).[11]

(8) *How much soot is deposited on each square inch of bread?*

Recent statistics can be found in the pamphlets, books, etc., of enthusiasts who wish to abate the Smoke Nuisance. We recommend them to adopt the simple expedient of abating the Factory-town Nuisance!

(9) *How many financial experts, politicians, eugenists, doctors, carters, farmers, journalists know that farmers sell their sheep wool for about 5d. a pound, and yarn-wool is sold across the counter at, say, 5s.[12] a pound?*

Good heavens!

The Cry of the English†

"PROBABLY NO English Government has ever been quite so near, in spirit and licence, to the atmosphere that we used to associate with the Tsar's government of Russia as the Government which ruled England for the first few years of the peace." To appreciate the value of this historical conclusion we must understand that "England" here means, not Ireland, nor Scotland, nor Wales, but England – that the "peace" is the peace which followed England's victory at Waterloo;[13] that the most prominent member of this Government was Lord Castlereagh,[14] who as leader of the House of Commons moved the suspension of the Habeas Corpus Act for England; and that the writers of this illuminating historical fact are J. L. Hammond[15] and Barbara Hammond in the last of their three works, *The Skilled Labourer.*

History As Officially Taught

The divorce between the officially taught history of schools or universities and the truth may be gauged by contrasting the sober, richly documented work of Mr. and Mrs. Hammond with any approved text-book of history.

The average English boy or girl has been taught – and very effectively taught – that the battle of Waterloo, not only symbolized England's home unity, strength, and prosperity, but ushered in an era of prosperity so great as to suggest the Millennium. It is always interesting to trace how history – that is, official history – has been called "a conspiracy against the truth." In the case of recent English history it is almost a mystery how upon an intelligent people could be foisted a view of what befell their grandparents which bore little or no relation to the truth except that

---

† *The Skilled Labourer (1760–1832).* By J.L. Hammond and Barbara Hammond. Longmans, Green and Co., pp. 397. 12s.6d. net.

of unabashed caricature. Perhaps one hidden reason may be suggested by the fact that Lord Castlereagh, who rode roughshod over Englishmen's liberties by suspending the Habeas Corpus, offered Labour and the clergy a bribe by allocating £1,000,000 for building new churches.

A Tragic Peace

Any page of *The Skilled Labourer* a proof of the historical findings which make the "Cry of the English" almost the most tragic note in the Europe of after-Waterloo.

Whilst the peace had brought about a return to industrial and financial prosperity shown by a vast increase in imports, exports and re-exports, the condition of the Workers, even the skilled workers, was worse than before the war. Thus "the Poor Weavers of Oldham" on their handbill could write: "After the Peace of Amiens...the wages of a journeyman would account to...15s. 9d. a week, and this was pretty near upon a par with other mechanics, and we maintained our rank in Society. ...During the last two years our wages have been reduced to so low an ebb that the journeyman's wages are...from 4s. 6d. to 5s. a week; and we appeal to your candour and good sense whether such a paltry sum be sufficient to keep the soul and body together" (p. 110).

Again, the Manchester *Political Register*[16] for January 4, 1817, gave a journeyman weaver's weekly receipt after deducting expenses as 2s. 5¼d.! "The *Political Register* declares that these budgets far exceed the average earnings of any considerable number. How do such people subsist?" it asks. "The answer is that they do not pay outgoings such as rent, and that they depend on parochial and private relief" (p. 344).

Industrial Magnates And Their Slaves

It may seem incredible that a people which war had just shown to be well-nigh indomitable should have borne this yoke without successful insurrection. But the wars which had been waged, perhaps truly enough to guarantee the freedom of Europe, played into the hands of the small number of clever profiteers and politicians who had no scruples about the slavery of England. War had merely shown these men and the mass of the rank and file that a small group of disciplined troops with munitions, and especially with artillery, could disperse a mob of thousands.

When Lamb[17] (afterwards Lord Melbourne) was supporting a Bill in the House of Commons in 1811 which made hosiery-frame breaking a capital felony, he tried to stifle the opposition of such men as Hutchinson and Sheridan[18] by "two ominous sentences. He declared that it was a delusion to suppose that the distress could receive my relaxation under the present unavoidable system; and that the fear of death had a powerful influence over the human mind" (p. 267).

This fear of death was used to such purpose by the industrial magnates and their politicians that the people gradually became quiet, especially when the hangings took place near the home of the victims, so that their wives and children might see the majesty and justice of the law!

English Rule In England

Spies, agents-provocateurs, packed juries, suborned witnesses, venal judges – all the furniture of tyranny which we have almost allowed as a monopoly of English rule in Ireland, was to be found in greater abundance, furthering English rule in England! It is significant that *The Skilled Labourer* closes its sober tragedy with a name which stirs the hate of Ireland almost equally with that of Cromwell. "To many historians the odium that surrounds the memory of Castlereagh is a mystery.... Historians who only think of England as an aristocracy in mortal conflict with Europe's tyrant attribute to spontaneous malice the hatred that haunted the Minister who defended her with such resolution and courage. But the mass of his countrymen remembered the War Minister who sent the armies to the Peninsula as the Minister who employed German mercenaries at the public flogging of English peasants; and the diplomat whose heart never failed him in the dark hours of the war with Napoleon, as the politician who regarded the poor of his country as he regarded the Jacobins of France. Hence in the Masque of Anarchy Sidmouth passes riding on his crocodile, and Eldon[19] weeping big tears that turn to millstones; but Castlereagh is followed by seven bloodhounds and throws them the hearts of his countrymen to chew" (p. 376).

"The Voice of the Irish"

Dublin Housing Conditions: Some Startling Facts

THE DUTY OF PREACHING on St Patrick, near whose grave I was born, recently took me for the twentieth time to one of the world's greatest books, an apostle's *Apologia pro vita sua*, the Confessions of St. Patrick. Once again I discovered that unique product of literature, only equalled in the Acts of the Apostles, the paragraph beginning in Latin entangled with Gaelic mannerisms: *"Et iterum post paucos annos."* Let my pen honour itself by writing it down word for word in a threadbare translation.

"Once more, after a few years, I was in Britain with my people. They welcomed me as a son, and by my love besought me that at least now after the many sorrows I had borne I would never leave them.

"And there, in the self-same place I saw in a vision of the night, a man whose name was Victoricus coming unto me from Ireland with letters beyond count. And he gave me one of them, and I read the beginning of the letter containing the Voice of the Irish.

"Whilst I was reading the beginning of the letter I seemed at the same moment to hear the voice of them who dwelt against the Wood of Foclut, nigh the Western Sea. With one voice, as it were, they cried out: 'Holy youth, we beseech thee, come once more into our midst and walk with us.'

"Thereupon was I greatly stricken at heart. I could read no more. And thus I awoke."

We of the twentieth century know what came of that dream and that awakening.

*****

I too have heard the "Voice of the Irish," the sob of my blood-kindred whom years of exile have not torn from my heart. It came to me in no vision of the night, but in that more awful form, a soul-withering vision of the day. Nor did it appear as a man whose name was as musical as Victoricus; but it came to me in the strident truthfulness of a "Report of the Departmental Committee appointed by the Local Government Board for Ireland to inquire into the Housing Conditions of the Working Classes of the City of Dublin."

You will say, "The Report is as dead as Finn Mac Coll.[20] It appeared a month ago." My reply is that I read it only twelve hours ago; and I promised God and St. Patrick, the two historic leaders of Irish thought, to do my little best to keep this Report from being strangled at birth.

Long ago I gave up reading penny dreadfuls and novels. They were not exciting enough. The purple patches I need, I find in blue books. An old Lancashire proverb says "There's nowt so odd as folk." Here is another proverb that can be launched from the same slipways: "There's nowt so mad as facts."

Bear with me, you who read this, if it is somewhat kneaded with grim humour. This is a trick I play with myself, to keep myself sane. The mad facts of this "Voice of the Irish" would almost mean a man's losing his reason or his soul.

Tenement Houses

We will set down some gruesome facts:

"1. Forty-five per cent. of the working population of Dublin live in tenement houses.

"2. There are 10, 696 families (37,552 persons) living in 2,288 houses that approach the border-line of being unfit for human habitation.

"3. There are 6,831 families (22,701 persons) living in 1,518 houses that are unfit and incapable of being made fit for human habitation.

"4. Of every 1,000 of population

Dublin has 339 in one room tenements.
Glasgow has 200 in one room tenements.

Liverpool has 54 in one room tenements.

Belfast has 6 in one room tenements.

"From this it will be seen that Dublin has by far the largest percentage of one-room tenements.

"5. The average number of persons in each one room tenement in Dublin is 3. 31, which is again the highest figure of the principal towns in the United Kingdom.

The Death Rate

"6. The death-rate in Dublin is higher than in any of the large centres of population in England, Wales or Scotland, and we fear that until the housing problem is adequately dealt with, no substantial reduction in the death-rate may be hoped for.

"7. The vast majority of the heads of families living in these tenement houses are earning less than 20s. a week.

"8. Of the tenement houses unfit or almost unfit for human habitation

1,146 are occupied by from 6 to 10 families.

59 are occupied by from 11 to 15 families.

1 is occupied by 24 families!

We have visited one house that was occupied by 98 persons.

"9. The tenement houses were evidently built to accommodate one family. They are exceedingly old structures, and are more or less in an advanced state of decay.

"10. 12,042 families (73,973 persons) occupy one room – an average of 6.1 per room. There are many tenements of seven or eight rooms with a family in each room, which contain a population of 40 and 50 souls.

*****

A Painful Passage

And now, patient reader, let me quote another passage which may bring a blush to your cheek whilst you read it, as it does to my cheek whilst I write it.

"Generally the water supply of the house is furnished by a single water-tap in the yard. The yard is common and the closet accommodation is to be found there, except in some few cases in which there is no yard, when it is found in the basement, where there is little light or ventilation. The closet accommodation is common not only to the occupants of the house, but to anyone who likes to come in off the street, and is of course common to both sexes.

"Having visited a large number of these houses in all parts of the city, we have no hesitation in saying that it is no uncommon thing to find halls and landings, yards and closets in a filthy condition, and in nearly every case human excreta are to be found scattered about the yards and on the floors of the closets and in some cases even in the passages. We are quite prepared to accept Sir Charles Cameron's[21] evidence, that the female inhabitants of the tenement houses seldom use the closets; indeed it would be hard to believe otherwise, as we cannot conceive how any self-respecting male or female could be expected to use accommodation such as we have seen."

Both the reader and the writer of these things must blush. Now the shame is not that these things should be published, but that they should be perpetuated by being hidden. These crimes against manhood and womanhood must be ended; and to be ended must be known

Dark Landings and Immorality

But there is even worse to come. We Catholics wage a relentless war against the politicians who would drive our children into the atmosphere of the purely secular school. We know that nothing kills so surely as an atmosphere. Listen!

"The entrance to all tenement houses is by a common door. The passage and stairs are common and the rooms all open directly off the passages or landings. It was stated in evidence before us by several witnesses, some of whom were clergymen whose duties bring them into close contact with tenement houses and who are therefore well qualified to speak, that the constantly open doors and want of lighting in the hall, passages and landings at night are responsible for much immorality. We fully endorse the evidence given by many witnesses that the surroundings of a tenement house in which there can be no privacy form the worst possible ATMOSPHERE for the upbringing of the younger generation, who, as one of the witnesses stated, acquire a precocious knowledge of evil from early childhood."

"The existing conditions of life in tenement houses in the city are both physically and morally bad, and there is urgent necessity for reform, which must have for its ultimate object the complete breaking up of the tenement system as it exists."

"The worst possible atmosphere! Some 20,000 families with some 60,000 children are bringing up these children...

'In the Worst Possible Atmosphere.'"

Writer and reader are again blushing, I hope; with a blush that menaces the makers of this iniquity with a *"Non licet esse vos."*[22] For this crime against childhood, this injustice against the most sacred property – namely, human life – must end.

No wonder the men of Dublin came out on strike. The wonder is that they bore their slavery so long. When I was a boy at an Irish school we learned to sing:

> O where's the slave so lowly
> Condemned to chains unholy
>   Who, could be burst
>   His chains at first,
> Would pine beneath them slowly?

Priests taught us to sing these verses, by singing them first themselves. If ever they were justified, then surely by the state of things under which the poor rot – I cannot say live – in our great centres of wealth.

The Dublin strike is over. Not everything the men did was well or rightly done. Yet the only blood spilled is their own. Starvation has harrowed none but them. But they shall know that the things from which they suffered and still suffer must end; for this "Voice of the Irish" has awakened many a soul, and is crying to the Father of the poor for vengeance.

*****

Yet would it ill-become me, a priest, and, therefore, a being dedicated unto peace, to end this message from the stunned heart with a wild cry for war. War may be inevitable. Yet for the moment let a priest beseech the rich to give us peace; not the inglorious peace that comes as the aftermath of a great massacre, but peace with plenty wherein the dream of a dead Vicar of Christ is realized. Let me close with...

Wise Words

from a source beyond suspicion. "If Labour discontent is not to be allowed to grow until it tears the country to pieces," says a special correspondent of the *Morning Post*,[23] "the individual employer, the firm, the joint-stock company, and the trust must prepare to take generally a more comprehensive view of their duties as leaders of industry. What the workers think when they are under a master whom they can respect and who takes a real interest in their welfare is the thought that will stand for the safety of the country at a crisis. What the workers think who are maddened by misfortune for which they blame their employers, no matter how unjustly, may be the thought that will bring down the Empire."

This is wisely written. God grant it may be wisely read.

Why Satan Wins

THREE INCIDENTS and a sheaf of statistics:
First incident, Tuesday, March 24:
At the Clerkenwell[24] County Court a man, against whom a possession order had been granted, said he had two children, and because of the children some agents had refused to put his name at all on their lists of waiting tenants.

> HIS HONOUR JUDGE PARFITT: I think it's a most abominable system. I cannot understand their doing it. A man with two children is, as a rule, a respectable man, and he should be encouraged rather than discouraged. I cannot speak too strongly of such conduct. Do you really mean to say that they have not taken your name down because you have got two children?
>
> WITNESS: That is so. As a matter of fact they told me they were not allowed to take the names of newly-married couples, because of possibilities.
>
> HIS HONOUR: There is a habit growing in this country which I think is very wicked, and that is to discourage families. It is a hardship for a man who is married, and it is the finish of family life.

*****

To the wife of a judgement debtor who said she had seven children the same Catholic Judge said:

> "In my judgement people with large families ought to be assisted. I don't agree with those who say people should not have large families. They ought to be assisted. I wish this expression of my opinion to be known. (To the woman): You are an honest woman and the mother of a large family, and I don't think you ought to be oppressed, but you ought to be assisted. I shall make an order for 5s. a month."

*****

The third incident is in striking contrast with its two predecessors:

> In Shoreditch[25] County Court, when a debtor told Judge Cluer
> that he had twelve children, the Judge was reported to have said:
> "Owing this money, you have no business to have twelve children.
> It is an injury to the country."

It will be agreed that the *prima facie* view of these incidents is disconcerting. The Shoreditch judgement has the air of being, not sentiment, but sound sense. The Clerkenwell judgement has the air of being, not sound sense, but sentiment; and sentiment which robs the community for the benefit of the thriftless individual.

I have called this the *prima facie* view or face-value of the incidents. And the taking of face-values is now so embedded in the national mind that it threatens to result in legislation which will unchurch the Decalogue. But it is only a face-value. The heart of the matter gives the lie to that face; and restores the Ten Commandments to their position as the only Agenda for a nation that wishes to survive by right of righteousness.

We must now meditate on a few statistics.

		Liverpool *	*St. Pancras*†	*Lambeth*‡
Population	... ...	829,881	214,400	308,000
Population per acre	...	40.8	80	75.5
One room families	...	11,064 (A.D. 1921)	12,811	10,074
Two room families	...	(19,000?)	17,584	14,851
Total families in one or two rooms each	...	(30,000?)	30,395	24,925

(a) These statistics should be not merely read but studied by all parliamentary secretaries, members of parliament, parliamentary and municipal voters, students of economics, scout and boys' brigade leaders, priests, Superiors of contemplative orders, bishops, magistrates, judges

---

* Report on the Health of the City of Liverpool during 1923, by the Medical Officer of Health, pp. 2 and 241.

† Report of the Medical Officer of Health for the year 1923, pp. 10 and 77.

‡ Report of the Vital and Sanitary Statistics for the Borough of Lambeth during the year 1923, p. 67 [and private letter to writer].

– in a word, all persons who love their birth-land and have an ordinary Englishman's fund of sound sense.

(b) Discussion is impossible, because reasoning is impossible with anyone who, on seeing these statistics, accuses the writer of them of being a Socialist, a Bolshevist, a Communist – or, for that matter, a Whig[26] or a Tory.[27] Facts, and especially first-hand facts, have no political bias. If these facts are Socialism or Toryism, then Socialism or Toryism is true, for these facts are true.

(c) It is not unlikely that there are in Liverpool about 30,000 families living each in one or two rooms. If we count four in each family, there are 120,000 of the citizens of Liverpool living with their families in one or two rooms. No wonder the Satanism of the Neo-Malthusian movement is winning quite easily.

(d) The statistics of the two London Boroughs have the great air of a doom!

On each acre of ground are housed some eighty persons! If we count only three (father, mother, and one child) in family, Lambeth[28] has some 75,000 souls living in one or two-roomed families.

St. Pancras has some 100,000 persons living in one or two-roomed families. No wonder Satan is winning almost without an effort.

(e) Denunciations of Neo-Malthusianism and praise of larger families seem almost blasphemous when unaccompanied by denunciations of the state of things revealed by the official reports of our Medical Officers of Health. It is quite clear that, theologically speaking, the state of things in which thousands of families live in one room is a proximate occasion of Neo-Malthusianism, just as residence in a house of ill-fame would be a proximate occasion of sexual sin. And our denunciations of a sinful system will seem, if not blasphemous, at least hypocritical, if not coupled with some earnest effort to end the system.

*****

Our meditation may end with what the masters of prayer call a spiritual bouquet from the *Rerum Novarum* of Pope Leo XIII:

> "There can be no question whatever that SOME REMEDY MUST BE FOUND AND FOUND QUICKLY for the misery and wretchedness pressing so heavily and so unjustly on the vast majority of the working-classes."

St. Thomas Aquinas on Town Planning

Being Chapter III From *De Regimine Principum*[29]

O F HOW THE CITY *which is to be built by the Sovereign should have a sufficiency of things, because without them the city cannot be perfect.* He distinguishes two kinds of sufficiency; but especially commends the first.

Now it is necessary that the site chosen for building the city should not only by its healthiness be fitted for keeping the citizens in health; but it should by its fertility suffice for their food. It is not possible for a multitude of men to dwell together where is no sufficiency of food. Hence, according to Aristotle,[30] when Xenocrates,[31] a most skilled architect, had proved to Alexander the Macedonian[32] that on a certain mountain a city of great beauty could be built, Alexander is said to have asked, if there were fields which could give the city a sufficiency of wheat. When he had found out that these were lacking, he replied that it would be folly to build a city in such a place; because as a new-born babe can neither live nor thrive without its nurse's milk, so likewise a city without a fullness of food cannot keep a crowd of people.

There are two ways whereby a city may have a sufficiency of things. The first is through the fertility of the place which yields abundantly everything needed for human life. The second is through trading, whereby the necessities of life are brought from foreign parts.

The first way is clearly seen to be the better. The more a thing is found to be self-sufficient the better it is; because what needs another is clearly wanting. A city whose neighbourhood gives the necessities of life in plenty possesses a sufficiency more fully than another city which depends on its trade with others. A city having its sufficiency from its own lands is nobler than one which abounds through trading.

Moreover, such a city would seem to be safer. The event of wars and the many mishaps of travel can easily hinder the transit of goods; and thus the city may perish for want of things.

Again, such a city would be fitter for civic life. When a city needs for its maintenance a multitude of merchants, it must put up with the continuous fellowship of foreigners. Now, according to what Aristotle says in his *Politics*, the fellowship of foreigners greatly corrupts the morals of citizens. The reason is because it must happen that foreigners, having been brought up on other laws and customs, act in ways very different from those of the citizens. Thus their example will draw the citizen to imitate them; and the good estate of the commonwealth will be disturbed.

Again, if the citizens themselves give themselves to trading, a way is opened to many vices. Since the desire of trading tends especially to gain; therefore through the use of trading avarice is enkindled in the hearts of the citizens; the result being that in the city all things will have their price; mutual trust will be at an end, doors will be opened to fraud, the common good will be despised, private good will be sought, zeal for virtue will wither because the honour of virtue will be given to all. Hence in such a city the civic life will be corrupted.

Moreover, the use of trading is very often contrary to the profession of arms. Traders, because they seek shady places, fly from toil. Moreover, in enjoying pleasures their courage grows less and their bodies become weakened and unfit for the toil of soldiering. Hence according to the civil laws trading is forbidden to soldiers.

Again, a city is likely to be the more peaceful the more seldom the citizens come together and the less they dwell within the town walls. The frequent meeting of men together begets the occasion of strife, and provides fuel for sedition; hence, according to the teaching of Aristotle, it is more fitting that the citizens should be occupied outside cities, than that they should dwell always within the city walls. But if the city is given up to commerce it is especially necessary that the citizens dwell within the city and follow their business. Therefore it is better for a city if it has a sufficiency of things from its own lands, than if it should be wholly exposed to commerce. Nevertheless, traders should not be wholly excluded from the city, because it is not easy to find any locality so abounding in all the necessaries of life that it does not stand in need of things brought from elsewhere. Moreover, when these same things superabound in the locality, this superabundance would in the same way become hurtful to many, if by the help of traders the things could not be carried to other localities. Hence the perfect city should use commerce moderately.

A Tale of Two Cities

New York City

ANNO DOMINI 1913 – New York City. This is the date and place of the first part of the Tale. It is such a horrible tale that I must give the exact circumstances, otherwise my readers may think I have made the tale "all out of my own head." But this would be too exquisite flattery for a head whose chief quality is an instinct for knowing where it can thieve to the best purpose.

Time, 3 p.m. Mrs. Marcella Dives, whose husband broke the meat ring at Porcopolis, is seen in 42nd St. – or is it 39th St. ? – shopping.

It is now six months since her first baby's birth. The heir apparent of the Dives millions is a fine boy. To see him is to want to cuddle him. Everyone envies his parents. As Judge Elijah Washington Elbow said to Reuben Yokohama Dives: "Say, Rube. You've been investing in Real Estate this time – sure!" But Mrs. Dives has evidently not the judicial mind of E. W. Elbow. At any rate, the fashionably-dressed shoppers of 42nd St.- or is it 39th St.? – see Mrs Dives and a nurse-woman and – the heir apparent. But the heir apparent is in the arms of the nurse. And in the arms of Mrs. Dives is a DOG!

*****

London City

The second part of the Tale is like to the first.

Anno Domini 1924 – London, Sunday, 10 a.m. A fine morning even for London. I am tramping from N.W. to S.W. I see a quietly-dressed elderly person pushing a perambulator. My heart leaps up as I think of the innocent babe, after three stormbound days in the nursery, at last released to the sun and air. I am prepared, as usual, to offer the beggar's alms of a smile to innocence in its perambulator; my theory being that the child by mere existence beggars my thanks, as do the snowdrops and the primroses.

As it is the first perambulator I have seen in my tramp from Hampstead to S. Kensington I am ready to be lavish with my smile. Indeed, I will smile so prodigally as to fill up every valley and wrinkle in my face, as I look upon this fortunate babe – whom a devoted and withal sensible mother is taking out to the tender mercies of the air and sun. I look at the perambulator, and see not my beloved innocence – but TWO PUGS!

*****

Babylon

To me, this is one tale – one horrible tale – one horrible, ghastly, grizzly nightmare of a beastly tale. But my friend, Professor Codex, says that by all the laws of Higher Criticism it is two tales, even as it is two cities. Yet he also propounds the alternative theory that it may be in essence one city and tale; and that the city is Babylon, and that the tale is Balaam and Josaphat.[33]

*****

But I know what you, gentle reader, are thinking in your heart. You are condemning Marcella and the nameless Lady of the Pugs. Now I beg of you not to be premature. Remember the golden epigram...

De Te Fabula Narratur.[34]

First of all, may we not be thankful that the Heir Apparent was not where the dog was – on his mother's icy bosom? A nurse's embrace was not the best thing for poor forlorn little Dives. But it was infinitely better than the dog-shelter. Give even a dog – even a she-dog – its due. Perhaps Marcella had been brought up and even educated (Lord, save us!) for the matrimonial market where women are taught all the arts (or tricks) for becoming a wife; and none of the secrets of being a mother. Perhaps in her humility Marcella felt fit only to nurse a dog. In that case how wide fall our arrows of indignation.

Who Shall Condemn?

Again, the Lady of the Pugs! Who are you and I, that we should condemn her? – especially that we should condemn her without a trial. Do we know the tragedy that filled her perambulator with pugs and not with cuddling babes? Alas! Babylon-on-Thames and Babylon-on-Hudson are so merciless to their citizens that many a young man and maiden who feel spurred to the adventure of founding a family are doomed to remain unwed – until they have found a house – or two rooms and the use of a kitchen! A bed-sitting room with a gas ring is not the bare minimum for a husband and a nursery. But it will do for breeding the smaller kinds of dogs. Moreover, dogs do not, like children, scratch the wallpaper and make loud noises on the floor – to the despair of the landlady.

More and moreover, some women must have something to love and fondle. If, therefore, they have no children of their own, who will blame them if, in secret, they kiss and fondle a litter of pugs? The hard critics who would stone this woman with the pug-perambulator would stone the poor folk who, unable to buy butter, try to make the best of margarine. Therefore he that is without sin amongst us let him begin the stone-throwing!

*****

The Villains Of The Piece

Again are not you and I, dear reader, the villains of this tragedy? Have we no sight beyond the tragic Marcella and the Lady of the Pugs; into that dark system which begets Marcellas and Ladies of the Pugs as infallibly as the mother of this litter begot the litter? The offal of the city – is it all our neighbour's doing; and not somewhat ours? Are we not in part our brother's keeper? When we love the things that freeze the mother's heart and dry her breasts, can we unabashed blame the dry breast and the frozen heart? Is Babylon-on-Thames and Babylon-on-Hudson, for us, the kingdom of heaven on earth?

Is Jerusalem our City – or Bethlehem?
Is Sion our mount – or Golgotha?
Is Mammon our God – or God?
Ipsi Viderimus![35]

The Problem of Unemployment

OR SOME TIME PAST I have been seeking to be loyal to the men who made the *Eye Witness* and the *New Witness*[36] by an endeavour to see and say the truth, on the hard matter of the unemployed. I had been haunted by the whole atmosphere of unemployment. The very word itself, "unemployment," so uncouth and so smug, seemed to be obsessed by some spiteful demon at war with the world.

Now, as an old professor whose job it has been to look words up and down, and to turn them inside out for the sake of Truth, my first duty seemed to be to trace the birth and heredity of the word. Archbishop Trench[37] had taught me that words no bigger than "yea" or "nay" stole the history of centuries. At once I betook myself to that Burke of English words, the Oxford Dictionary, only to find that the giants responsible for the dictionary had not yet reached "unemployment." Amen!

I then betook myself to Lloyd's Encyclopedic Dictionary, alas, full of the memories of one of the greatest scholars I ever knew, who recommended its scholarship to my youth. My sense of obsession became the deeper when on consulting the generous pages of the dictionary I could find no mention of the word, though the work was published in 1895! Then, still in search for the parentage of "unemployment" and thinking that, although now a naturalized English word, it may have been begotten across the seas, I consulted their great word book, Funk and Wagnalls,[38] 1903. There, to be sure, I ran my quarry to earth. But the American lexicographers did not exorcise the obsession with their laconic note: "Unemployment: very rare."

Now it has always seemed to me that if we are to follow Plato in awaiting great social changes when a nation changes the songs it sings,[39] we must await or recognize still greater changes when a nation changes the words it uses. If "unemployment" is such a new word that only thirty years ago it was unknown to one of the greatest of our English lexicographers, and only eighteen years ago it was considered very rare by one of the most alert of our American lexicographers, some mystery must be behind the world-wide vogue which it has in the year of Our Lord nineteen hundred and twenty-five.

Thirty years ago if England had been covered with the present wave of "unemployment" it would have discussed the matter in some other word or words. Thus in 1890 that very acute master of men and words, General Booth,[40] founder of the Salvation Army, wrote his book *In Darkest England and the Way Out*. He deals with the present evil overwhelming these islands. But the special chapter dealing with it is picturesquely and significantly headed, "Out-of-Works."

It is then a matter of deep concern that in some thirty years both the leaders and the rank and file of the working-classes are discussing their present straits not as a problem of poverty or even as a problem of work, but as a problem of employment. We need hardly remind our readers how many ideas and assumptions are latent in the word "employment" which are not to be found in the word "work." The word "work," as such, implies a relation merely to a thing. The word "employment" implies this work-relation to a thing, but adds a new relation to person or employer.

Now for the purpose of clear economic thinking we have misgivings even about the words "work, worker, out-of-work, workless, worklessness, etc." But we have far more misgivings about the series of words "employed, employee, employment, unemployment, etc."; for these have all the assumptions and ambiguities of the first series and many more of their own.

It is not all who, at first sight, can see the assumptions of such a phrase as "the Problem of Unemployment." It will be easy for them to do so if they think of other evils and of their remedies. Thus if we speak of the evil of slavery, emancipation of the slave is the only remedy, and the emancipator is the chief benefactor. If we speak of the unfed and of underfeeding, food is the only remedy, and the food-giver is the chief benefactor. Again if we speak of the uneducated and of under-education, education is the only remedy, and the educator is the chief benefactor

In the same way, if we speak of the evil of unemployment, then employment is the only remedy, and the employer is the chief benefactor! It is clear that this assumption is one which should be challenged by all who see in the social ethics of Christianity a hunger and thirst after that virtue of justice which gives everyone his due. When such an authority as the *Rerum Novarum* wishes States to have as their policy the extension of the Ownership System, and therefore the diminution of the Wage System, it would seem a dangerous policy to express our modern remedies in terms of extended employment.

It cannot be too often repeated that what is the matter with the "unemployed" is not their unemployment but their poverty. The present crisis is an evil of Poverty, economically almost entirely reducible to an evil of wrong production. Yet through the prolonged gas-attack of the Wage System even Labour's elect seem to be deceived. Thus J. R. Clynes[41] writes under the title, "Unemployment" (*The Times*, October 30, 1922): "At present the nations of Central Europe are unable to buy because they have nothing to pay with, and the loss of their custom is one of the most fruitful causes of unemployment not only in Great Britain but in the United States." According to Mr. Clynes one main trouble is that the foreigner has no money to buy our goods. On this diagnosis the remedy is clear: "A generous attempt to finance the foreigner may yet prove to be our cheapest and most effective road to salvation." The economics of this does not seem over clear. But Mr. Clynes recommends it to his fellow working men by the following plea: "This scheme...would bring into the service of the State, *without cost to the taxpayer,* the best financial brains, skill, and experience which the country possesses. Such a contribution given voluntarily by the bankers and insurance experts of the country would go far to convince the workers of the genuineness the proposals." These proposals are no doubt quite genuine and sincere; as were the proposals made by Dick Turpin[42] to his clients. But are they sound? Are they perhaps an attempt not to be richer but to feel richer by transferring our last sixpence from our vest pocket to our coat packet? Are they a pitiful effort, not to be stronger, but to feel stronger by gnawing our own arm?

We leave these questions to the wisdom of our readers, confessing that the word "unemployment" haunts us still with its callous assumption that the cure for our *delirium tremens*[43] is a further draught of the poison which has been our undoing.

A Challenge to Modern Industrial Methods

AT THE RISK of appearing to be a fanatic, I venture to suggest that the time has come for balancing the Profit and Loss Account of modern industrial methods. Such a suggestion should be welcomed by all the upholders of these methods, if for no other reason than that stock-taking and balancing are amongst the most obvious features of modern industrialism. Moreover, the modern industrial system, with its machinery, factory, and factory-town, has had at least a century's growth. We have, therefore, sufficient data, no doubt, for an economist accountant to draw up a fairly accurate balance sheet.

The aim of such a balance sheet would be to show whether or not modern industrial methods have succeeded in reaching the end they aimed at in the beginning of their existence. It would be no part of the enquiry to investigate the moral effects of industrialism. This investigation, which, of course, would be of first importance, would demand not an economic but an ethical expert – a rare craftsman. But the enquiry we propose would be confined, naturally enough, to merely economic channels. For example, without enquiring whether the transfer of the wool trade from home to factory resulted in a lower moral or political standard, we would enquire whether nowadays after a century of factory production the average family of today surpassed the average family of say 1700 A.D. or 1200 A.D. in the quantity and quality of his woollen goods.

(a) Let us take the most provocative head of enquiry, the railways. Let us be foolhardy enough to challenge our modern railway system as an industrial instrument.

We shall have to enquire not merely into the patent fact that between certain points, say London and Birmingham, transit has become quicker. In our proposed balance sheet we can certainly enter this item on the credit side. There are, doubtless, many more items to be set down beside it under the head of credit. But our chief duty in this article is to suggest that whereas for a hundred years the credit side has been very carefully posted up, there have been few or no entries on the debit side. Yet in this matter of transit, *we must consider how the Railway System has facilitated, not the saving of time, but the loss of time.* In a simple agricultural community with its simple agricultural villages or towns, where everyone lived in his own homestead or worked in his own home, there was little or no time lost in going to work. Ten minutes at most of pleasant walks took a man to the work of the day. But nowadays by the help of Railways, men can spend as much as two or four hours a day travelling by train. Thus "Brighton and Eastbourne Expresses" are but expensive ways of losing time.

Consider, in particular, the Tubes![44] To many naive minds these underground thoroughfares are almost the fine flower of modern civilization; which Londoners point out with pride to their country cousins. Yet was there ever a more infernal contrivance for getting about from one place to another? Tube-travelling is like travelling in a coal cellar, with second-hand air and in such a din that human speech is possible only to throats of brass. No wonder men forced to spend a good portion of their day in these abodes of reek and din, far from human converse, bury their heads and minds in the morning or evening press to devour daily rations of news as one of the easiest and cheapest ways of forgetting what manner of men they are, and what an inhuman manner of transit they are forced to adopt for the joy of living out of London.

Take the transit of food. Railways facilitate the loss of time – and food. I quite agree that for a generation or thereabouts the average person was possibly benefited by railways bringing him more or cheaper food than his grandfather. Railways, however, facilitate not merely quick transit but the quick growth of great towns; and great towns mean useless transit and scarce food.

There is not space to deal with this matter. But in spite of bananas and cotton goods, let anyone try to make an accurate scientific contrast between the quantity and quality of food obtainable by an ordinary joiner or ploughman in the year 1219 and an ordinary London joiner or taxi-driver in 1919. The investigator may end his investigation by applying to railways Admiral Fisher's[45] advice about the Fleet, "Scrap the lot!"

At any rate two facts are at least significant; if not symbolical. In 1219 foreign wine – a most natural and pleasant drink – was cheap enough for working men. Now it has become so dear as to be within the means only of the rich. Secondly: I was told in Galway,[46] one of the greatest salmon-catching centres of these islands, that all the salmon sold in Galway fish-shops, had a chequered career. First of all it had been caught in Galway – then it had been packed and sent by train and boat to London – next it had been unpacked – lastly it had been repacked and resent by train and boat to Galway! Yet most people think of railways as essentially and undeniably economical!

(b) Consider factory production, known to us all as multiple or quantitative production; it is agreed even amongst the friends of this system that the system kills qualitative production. Machinery cannot give us the best things, but it gives us, they say, a great many of the worst things, or, at least, a great many of the second-best things. What it lacks in quality, it seeks to make up in quantity.

Now for the ordinary sane man this would be the end of factory production. No one would calmly say that in his attitude towards life he was quite deliberately sacrificing the best to the second best. Yet this must be the attitude of those who hope to keep the factory system in being.

But we, though we deny that factory production is qualitative production go on to challenge the assertion that it is quantitative production, at least, of the primary necessities of life.

It is almost a platitude to suggest that no factory has the power to produce the necessities of life; at least, they can manipulate and modify material supplied to them. For the production of milk no machine equals a cow or a goat; for the production of flour no machine equals a head of wheat; for the production of beer no machine equals malt and hops.

Just as railways, which are praised for facilitating transit, should be challenged for facilitating useless transit, so also factory production, which claims to have made things more procurable should be challenged for making the necessities of life less procurable by the majority of mankind – i.e., the working classes. Cobbett[47] showed this fact to England at the beginning of the 19th century. Yet his grateful country contrived to discredit its almost unique truth-teller, because he would not flatter her with a falsehood. But the truth of Cobbett's diagnosis has become true and more undeniable after a hundred years of factory production. To test the truth we have to think not of factory production in general, nor of the production of unnecessary things, say, like motor cars, big guns, margarine, and the whole diabolic hierarchy of canned substitutes; but of such primary and indispensable things as boots, milk, bread, meat, clothes and houses. These things are not more within the reach of the working man than they were. They are so far from his reach that he is content merely to touch them or to accept "substitutes" and rations.

To put it another way. None of the necessaries of life really come by factory production; but from the land. Now in spite of motor-ploughs and chemical manures land does not produce more than it did (in proportion to the population) but less than it did. The figures for our own country are appalling. Mr. Lloyd George[48] supplied them in his speech on Agricultural Reconstruction, and told us that since 1870 (Educationalists, please note) 46,000,000 acres of arable land have gone out of cultivation; since 1871 the numbers of people engaged on the soil has decreased by 700,000 (of whom 600,000 are men) making with their families some 3,000,000 people. All this decrease in production has taken place, although the experts assured the Prime Minister that the £150,000,000 worth of food we buy abroad might be raised in our own country.

Surely this is enough to make some expert challenge the demand for increased production, that is, for increased factory production by a counter demand for an economic balance sheet. It will then be seen that our modern industrial methods have indeed produced *more wealth for the few who control, without in any way producing wealth*. Indeed, whilst some men have become richer, other men have become poorer, so that the State should no longer be called the Commonwealth but the Common Poverty.

The Decay of Dancing

A CERTAIN NOBLE BOOK, which has many full pages on banqueting and dancing, tells the story of a younger son, a spendthrift, who left the country for the town, his home for hotels, his father for fellow spendthrifts. His mood of folly lasted until he found himself a swineherd, so foodless as to envy the swine their swill. Wisdom came to him when he recalled the great fullness of things in his father's house that even the hired servants had more bread than they could eat. The story of this younger son comes to an end fitly in a great banquet of welcoming compounded of a number of things, to wit: a father's kisses, a first robe, a ring, new shoes, the fatted calf, eating, drinking, music and a dance.

Now it has seemed to some authentic seers that the greater tragedy is not that of the younger son; but of the elder son. This man who had led such a blameless life as to have left no record on the annals of the local court, suddenly unveiled the hidden flaw of his soul on the occasion of the great dance given to welcome his younger brother. With the awful precision and simplicity of a doom, it is written: "AND HE WAS ANGRY AND HE WOULD NOT GO IN"! He therefore stayed outside in the danceless dark of the night This is a horrible beginning of tragedy, which makes his further fate haunt us even in dream. Of that fate you and I, gentle reader, know nothing. But a seer I once met shepherding his flock in the Cotswolds,[49] said that after forty-seven years searching for what befell the elder son, he found him in the next chapter of St Luke as the general secretary to whom we owe the famous phrase, "To dig I am not able; to beg I am ashamed." But this shepherd seer, who was once in his wild days a Scripture Professor at Cambridge, added, "The text has shifted. I feel it ought to be 'To beg I am not able. To dig I am ashamed. Therefore I will steal.'"

Now to return to dancing. All of us who tremble at the doom of the elder son realize that the beginning of evil was begotten or revealed by his attitude towards the dancing that welcomed his brother's return to home and sanity. Hereupon, as befits the subject, we may examine the conscience of our contemporaries towards dancing, lest some evil should befall them as great as befell the elder son. To begin with, dancing is of a nature so human, and, therefore, so divine, that *il Beato Angelico*,[50] who knew the ways of Heaven if ever a painter did, has painted Paradise as a dance of angels with men, and men with angels.

When Adam and his wife Eve walked through the paradise of earth, the birds made music in the trees. To that music the feet of the happy two wedded a dance. Song and dance ended when the serpent came; for in hell there is no song, but only noise; nor any graceful dance, but only hideous grimaces.

I have a thought that the dance, which met its death in the Garden with the coming of the serpent, came to life again when Adam took his first-born in his arms and dandled him in sheer joy of fatherhood. It was born again when Adam, reaped with song the first autumn fruits of seeds he had sown with tears in the darkness of winter. It is always a dance I see when I look upon the sewer casting his seed or the ploughman turning over the furrow, or the harvester swinging his sickle. Again, what can a man do but dance when he hears the flail song in threshing time – or the music of the churn when butter is a-making?

Only those who, through love of things as against tokens of things, live on the land know what the dance is in its heart and being. Only away from the compression of the town have the feet of men and women room enough to shake off the divine fire of dancing. At the crossways they can dance when the sun or the moon is up. When rain falls or the storm is master of the sky and earth, each homestead has a threshing floor where the feet of these who dance come into their own on the noiseless clay.

A thousand pleas for dancing are found by those who live on the land. No men and women make such wedding feasts, or can find such good cheer to give their guests, or have such spacious places for the ritual of the dance. Mostly the dance is a lovely liturgy fitly carried out in the hallowed building of the home. The young and old take part in it; the young as actors, the old as judges and spectators. There in the sanctuary of home this ritual dance is a social thing, of as much joy to them who quietly sit and watch as to them who nimbly play their part in the thing or act itself.

Alas! as men have given up the land for the city, and home and homestead, for "rooms" or "flats," even their dancing is under sentence of death. Where in Bayswater or Kilburn or Rotherhithe[51] is there any home where a wedding dance can be housed? Just as men's city eyes, that are now so far from green fields or the seas must be content with the "films" of these good things which they find to their cost in a Coliseum or Palladium (save the mark!), so when their feet are hungry and thirsty for the dance must they buy their place and perhaps their partner in some hall where the divine thing, which the blessed Angelico of Fiesole painted as the occupation of heaven, is set on foot by someone keen on the making of money! Industrialism has turned full wheel when even the divine act of dancing is but a device for increasing dividends.

The better sort of men and women lull their town restlessness for the dance by paying to see the professional dancer. Against these artistes of a noble art we will allow no word to be said. But we would allow almost any word to be said against the state of things that has made it necessary for some of these artistes to make such gains by selling their art. When every home was a homestead and every homestead had its kitchen floor, or its spinning floor, or its threshing floor, and every lad or lass could hope to dance at countless village feasts or wedding banquets, there was no need for them to be spectators, being themselves actors. But now the spinning wheels having gone from the kitchen, the flail from the threshing floor, the ploughman from the furrow, and dancing from the land that dances in the autumn breeze, we must drug our grief by paying the professional to show us our dead selves in a maze of artificial art. R.I.P.

The Economics of a Riot

An Open Letter To A Hand Worker

THE DOINGS AND SAYINGS of the past few months, and especially the sayings and doings of the last Trade Union Congress, gave my soul no rest until chance led me to a scene which afforded a clue to recent history. My old teacher of history had counselled me to make books of a thousand years old the substance of my reading and to take the daily gossip of civilization merely as an aftermeat. In his boldness, which ensured his slow access to honour and emolument, he even went so far as to affirm, on oath, that if I sought for the real foundations of the philosophy of history I should find more in any one of the books of the New Testament, say, in the Acts of the Apostles, than in all the yearly output of the Universities. Needless to say that when I heard such statements from his lips I took them for talkativeness or folly. Time has shown that he was of the race of prophets.

Demetrius The Silversmith

It was not, therefore, wholly by chance, or only by such chance as befalls a man who of habit chooses the best, that I fell upon a passage you may know almost by heart. Here it is:

> Now at that time there arose no small disturbance about the way of the Lord. For a certain man named Demetrius, a silversmith, who made silver temples for Diana, brought no small gain to the craftsmen. Whom he calling together, with the workmen of like occupation, said:
>
> "Sirs, you know that our gain is by this trade. And you see and hear that this Paul by persuasion hath drawn away a great multitude not only of Ephesus, but almost of all Asia, saying. 'They are not

gods which are made by hand.' So that not only this our craft is
in danger to be set at nought; but also the great temple of Diana
shall be reputed for nothing. Yea, and her majesty shall begin to be
destroyed whom all Asia and the world worshippeth."

Having heard this word, they were full of anger and cried
out:

"Great is Diana of the Ephesians!"

And the whole city was filled with confusion (Acts xix 23-29).

Written For Our Instruction

You will agree that the scene is picturesque, and even dramatic.
It is the first conflict between the Christian Apostles and Organized
Labour. Every detail of the scene would seem to have been written for
our instruction.

Perhaps you may have remarked that this first conflict between
Christian priests and Organized Labour was itself organized. It did not
spontaneously grow up between Paul, the tent-maker of Tarsus, and the
silver-craftsmen of Ephesus. These metal-workers would probably have
left Paul undisturbed to his new craft of word-sowing if they had not
been carefully engineered into a riot.

The Worker And The Capitalist

Moreover, this riot of organized labour was organized by Demetrius the silversmith; in plain English, by a capitalist. For the moment
I have not a word of ill or good to say of capitalists. But I put it to you
as a man to man: "How would you, Socialist and a craftsman, like to
be engineered into riot against religion – by a capitalist? Would you not
remember the old proverb of Virgil: 'Timeo Danaos'?[52] Would you not
fear even for your own little holding when a capitalist goaded you to pull
down your brother's? Would you not feel that you were your brother's
keeper; or, at least, would you not feel afraid when asked to be your
brother's hangman?" When I was a younger man I once heard an older
and wiser man say to some workmen: "Men, when a rich man says to you,
'Down with Jesus Christ!' or 'Down with religion!' or 'Down with the
priests!' keep a sharp eye on your holding or your bits of sticks, for the

rich man is going to filch them from you." My wise master had thought
a lot about Demetrius the silversmith.

The Power Of Demetrius

Haven't you an instinct that this "Demetrius, a silversmith, who
made silver temples for Diana, and brought no small gain to the craftsmen," was a sweating employer, a ruthless profiteer? He is of that white-
wash-loving class. The poor wretches whom he employed to make silver
temples for Diana, and incidentally to make silver shekels for himself, are
so wholly his slaves that he can employ them to make a riot at his bidding.
What man of them would have dared to say to him: "Well, sir, this Paul
hasn't said more than he thinks the truth. Ours is a free country. Nobody
need follow Paul's way of thinking unless he likes. So I ain't going to
make a row." Had the poor wretch said this, he would soon have had a
week's notice to quit work, and face starvation.

Not Diana, But Mammon

No doubt you and I are at one in despising the way in which
Demetrius the capitalist engineered religion. We should both have deep
sympathy and respect for the simple folk in Ephesus and elsewhere to
whom Diana was a real goddess whom they served, loved, or feared. Nor
should we part company if one or the other of us found an excuse for the
simple faith which thought that the god they worshipped would conde-
scend to dwell in the work of their hands. But it is impossible to stomach
the blasphemous hypocrisy of this Demetrius who trades on Diana of
the Ephesians, as if she were his deity, and all the while he worships not
Diana, but Mammon.

A Bad Speech

No doubt the speech he made that day on behalf of Diana at Ephesus hit its mark. The applause had been carefully prearranged. The spontaneous outbursts had probably been rehearsed. But the speech was a bad
speech from beginning to end. Its one redeeming point was that, in spite

of Demetrius's efforts to the contrary, the speech revealed the speaker. The truth would out. Matters of first importance came first: "Not only this our craft is in danger to be set at nought, but also the temple of the great Diana shall be reputed for nothing." It was as if he said: "I shall lose £5,000; and, of course, God will be dishonoured." The juxtaposition of these two sentiments in the one sentence is a subtle blasphemy impossible to the simple craftsmen whom he was leading meekly and tamely to the shambles. And this blasphemy is still a feature of the economic world.

The man had no vision. He was thereby no fit company for these craftsmen; for these men and their brothers in all ages have eyes for ever troubled with a vision beyond the light of common day. For this reason they seldom commit suicide, but are commonly led to slaughter.

Imagine the fatuousness of the fool who, hearing Paul of Tarsus proclaim the world's good news of Jesus of Nazareth, thought of Paul and of Jesus only as a disturber of economic equilibrium! Imagine how clogged were the eyelids of this profiteer-employer who did not realize the wealth of silver-work and gold-work that the world in its gladness would command for the head and hands, and even the feet, of the Crucified!

Organizing Servile Craftsmen

Yet Demetrius was no fool; or not altogether a fool. He was mad, like Hamlet, only when the wind was in certain points of the compass. His was the madness of those reputed clever men who fix the end of life where no end is. In reaching that end he showed only wisdom; or that craftiness which often shows better than wisdom. He had succeeded in clearing his chief enemy out of the way by organizing his servile crafts-men into opposition against this new world-ambitioning spiritual power which could and would challenge his injustice towards his craftsmen.

Fortunately or unfortunately for his craftsmen, once he had made his fool's choice of serving, not God nor Diana, but Mammon, he served the vulgar god of his choice with all the zeal of a devotee. In other words, he had chosen to go to hell; and, as Sir Thomas More said of another man of like craft and folly, "he bought hell dearer than saints buy Heaven." Moreover, he was trying to go there with company.

But knave or fool that he was, is he any fit master, or law-maker, or leader for the men whose salvation is in the work of their hands?

The Economics of the Exodus

THERE IS A LIKELIHOOD that the Bible, which, as a book of dogma and morals, has largely lost its hold upon modern minds, may be able to recover its hold as a book of economics. Nor is this to be wondered at; unless, indeed, men fail to realize that those dogmas and ethics which yield no fruit of sound economics can hardly be accepted as themselves sound. St Thomas Aquinas[53] in the thirteenth century was among the first to recognize in the Mosaic code of laws a collection of economic principles, which was of first importance to the Europe of his day. His work in summarizing and, if we may be allowed the phrase, in codifying the Mosaic laws has made his *Summa Theologica* one of the indispensable introductions to scientific economics. It is, then, in the spirit and with the principles of our master that we venture to make an economic commentary on the Mosaic Exodus from Egypt.

Certain steps in the history of this Exodus are best told in the words of the only first-hand authority we have: to wit, the Pentateuch:

> "Then Joseph went in and told Pharaoh, saying: My father and brethren, their sheep and their herds, and all they possess, are come out of the land of Canaan; and behold they stay in the land of Gessen...
>
> "And he asked them: What is your occupation?
>
> "They answered: We thy servants are shepherds; both we and our fathers. . . .
>
> "But Joseph gave a possession to his father and his brethren in Egypt in the best place of the land in Ramesses, as Pharaoh had commanded."†

Object of Pharoah's Generosity

1. The motive behind Pharaoh's generosity towards the Israelite people may well be left undecided. Sovereigns in search of autocratic

---

† Gen. xivii I – II

power have commonly called in the aid of foreign mercenaries. The special privileges granted by Pharaoh to this little hardy shepherd race were likely to provide him with a group of loyal supporters who could be trusted in an hour of revolution.

2. The Israelite people are represented as a shepherd race, not altogether unacquainted with stable tillage, yet depending for their livelihood mainly on their flocks. They were as closely related as men could be to the land, from which alone the world's real wealth must come.

3. This little shepherd people, strangers to Egypt, whom Pharaoh, had preferred to his own subjects, could hardly fail to become an object of jealousy, and even of hatred.

Joseph and the Native Egyptians

Moreover, Joseph, the Israelite, who was responsible for the importation of these strangers, had proved himself one of the greatest oppressors of the native Egyptians.

> "From that time unto this day, in the whole land of Egypt the fifth part is paid to the king, and it is become as a law, except the land of the priests, which was freed from this covenant."†

In this phrase is summarized the exhaustive record of how Joseph, taking advantage of an alleged famine, brought into Egypt the conditions of the Servile State. His special treatment of the priestly class was a diplomatic move of such success that it has had its re-echoes in more modern times.

> "In the meantime there arose a new king over Egypt that knew not Joseph. And he said to his people: Behold the people of the children of Israel are numerous and stronger than we. Come,, let us wisely oppress them, lest they multiply; and if any war shall arise against us join our enemies, and having overcome us, depart out of the land.
>
> "Therefore he set over them masters of the works, to afflict them with burdens, and they built for Pharaoh, cities of tabernacles, Phithom and Ramesses"‡

---

† Gen. xivii 26.   ‡ Exod. i 8–11.

1. The inevitable did not tarry in its course. Soon there arose into open opposition the sullen jealousy which had been given to the strangers of Israel. Questions of public safety were urged to curb the power of this people whose shepherd morality had multiplied them in contrast with the over-civilized Egyptians.

A Political Problem

2. The Israelite question became an urgent matter of politics, perhaps even of party politics. The party of public safety had a good deal to say against the numeric growth of this alien race who could not be trusted to take sides with Egypt against enemies who were of their own kith and kin. Whether or not the Israelite question became a party cry, it is clear that the public opinion of Egypt was wholeheartedly on the side of Pharaoh and his policy of coercion.

Organized Town-Planning

3 It speaks volumes for the thoroughness of a country whose men of science had invented reinforced concrete many centuries before the Christian era, that it has also been a pioneer in organized town-planning. Phithom and Ramesses, these "cities of tabernacles," seem to have been but earlier models of our "garden cities," which are often taken to be the last word of modern civilization.

If the Code of Hammurabi,[54] with its recognition of "commercial travellers," betokens a very early development of the great commercial houses, we may ask if these cities of tabernacles do not argue some elementary form of industrialism almost equivalent to "mass production." It would seem all the more likely when we read that the Egyptians made the life of the Israelites "bitter with hard works in clay and brick."† The clay or brick unit of construction is perhaps the outward visible sign of a civilization that has become thoroughly unitized and industrialized. No one can fail to see this in our own times, if he looks round the newly-built parts of an industrialized town.

---

† Exod. i 14.

"And the king of Egypt spoke to the midwives of the Hebrews commanding them: When you shall do the office of midwives to the Hebrew women, and the time of delivery is come, if it be a man-child, kill it; if a woman, keep it alive. But the midwives feared God and did not do as the king of Egypt had commanded, but saved the men children."†

We are not altogether surprised that the organization extended itself even to the midwifery service. The text allows us to think it possible that the mid-wifery service was part of a government department.

Eugenic Birth Control

It is equally obvious that one of the chief functions of this government midwifery was to keep down the growth of undesirables. Eugenic birth-control is at least as old as Pharaoh; not as recent as Francis Galton![55] Any Egyptian who loved his birth-land could but bewail the doom of a country which could keep alive only its new-born girls.

Two questions here become pertinent:

I. Is there any record of a people remaining on the land and shunning cities, or going out to the land by quitting cities, without a religious motive?

II. Is it in the nature of things that only a religious motive can keep people on the land or can send them to the land from the cities?

I. As regards the first, we are still seeking for some historical records of a town civilization being changed into a land civilization by a non-religious motive. Again and again town civilizations have been changed into land civilizations. Tyre and Sidon,[56] once the emporia of the East, became folds for sheep. Babylon and Nineveh[57] are still the haunt of desert beasts of prey. Again and again wolves have prowled in the grass-grown streets of Rome.

Passing of Great Cities

Not some great cities, but all great cities, have passed away. But the movement from city life to the land has not come by peaceful or warlike

---

† Exod. i 17.

revolution from within. It has come by warlike invasion from without. Inner strife has assuredly lessened the unity of the city civilization. But it has only prepared the victim for its sacrificial destruction by the hand of the foreign invader. Yet only the city, and not the country, can be destroyed. There may be an end to Paris, or London, or Rome, but not to France, or England, or Italy. Indeed, in the hour when the city is given over to destruction its fugitives are finding in their Alma Mater, the earth, that education in the essentials of life which can come only from direct contact with the realities of land and sea and sky.

II. Our second question may not be patient of an undeniable answer. Yet if instincts, stabilized by history, may justify certitude, we are strongly of opinion that human nature being what Baptism teaches us that it is, religion alone can lead men out of the cities to the land, or keep them on the land in spite of the lure of cities. These are some of the reasons in which our instinct finds expression.

(a) The land is well-suited for wealth-making, but ill-suited for mere wealth-getting. Land-workers and their faithful companions, hand-workers, give the community real wealth in the things they cultivate or make from the land. The city dweller, divorced from real wealth, becomes an expert in token wealth.

Attractions of the City

Now, by the skilful use of tokens in the great gamble of wealth-getting the city-dweller can amass wealth – and often real wealth – more easily than can the land-worker. It would therefore be abnormal, unnatural, or supernatural and divine if the city dweller went back to the life on the land.

(b) Moreover, the town-dweller can divide his life much more easily and commonly into work and leisure; or, as some would say, into work and pleasure. On the land there is not the same place for leisure. Nor call leisure be allotted with all the precision of a timetable, Beasts and the climate owe little allegiance to time-tables. All this makes the truth in the proverb, "A farmer's work is never done." Town-dwellers find the city organized to give them a thousand pleasures for their hours of leisure. Thus it would be abnormal and divine if the town-dweller left his pleasure-filled leisure for the work-laden life on the land.

Life of the Land-Worker

(c) Again, the life of the land-worker being a direct relation to things, is also a direct conflict with nature. It is not easy for man to deal with nature in all her moods. One or other of the four seasons of the year will usually find out what is weakest in man's physical strength. Now, town-life has ten thousand contrivances for dulling the sharp point of nature's fang. The "cities of tabernacles," or garden cities of the Egyptians, gave the rich every luxury for tempering the fierceness of an Egyptian summer. As for the mere labouring poor, life on the land was for them not so much unendurable as impossible. The very poor are everywhere a city-fungus of the very rich. No agricultural civilization has ever produced them. But city life, with its unstable industrialism, not only produces and fosters them for its self-existence, but keeps them within the city by unfitting them for life on the land. No wonder that the poor Hebrew proletariat of Pharaoh's brickyards found direct contact with the land far from their liking The Egyptian "flesh-pots" were remembered with regret, even after the daily meal of Heaven-sent manna. If for a moment we are at a loss to realize how a people set free from national thraldom could even regret their past ill-fortune, we have but to imagine what would happen if some social leader had sufficient influence nowadays to lead a colony from one of our cities out to the land.

Enthusiasts of the Last Century

Now and again during the last century and a half social enthusiasts have tried to follow in the way of Moses by founding land-colonies of men and women gathered from city life. These efforts have done little else than provide arguments against brainless enthusiasm. As years go on the chances of success for such enthusiasts become steadily less. The men and women of the London of today are further removed both from the land and from the qualities needed for land-life than the men and women of a hundred years ago. Cobbett's Cockney had more of the land-colonist in him than the men and women who today travel to and from the City by motor-bus or tube. It is, then, abnormal or divine to lead dwellers in a city back to the land. That Moses did this divine thing, and did it with full acknowledgement of the divine initiative and help, is his claim to a unique position in human history.

A Great Turning Point

It makes the great turning point in the chosen people an economic turning point of the world. We are not sure that even Moses was able to make his fellow Hebrews forget the damnable conveniences of city life. A long sojourn in the desert might have been expected to content them with the land flowing with milk and honey. Yet no sooner had they entered the land of great promises fulfilled than the remembrance of Egyptian city civilization so discontented them with the land that they coveted a king and a kingly city. God in His anger gave them their desires. With Saul, David, Solomon as their kings, and with Jerusalem as their royal city, the little God-called people had hardly begun to fulfil their mission when they began their decay.

The End of the Wage System

> The law should favour ownership. Its policy should be to induce
> as many as possible of the humbler classes to become owners.
>
> —Pope Leo XIII, *Rerum Novarum.*

To understand the meaning and feel the force of these words of
Pope Leo XIII we must contrast them with words which he used elsewhere in the same Encyclical: "Working men have been surrendered, all
isolated and helpless, to the hard-heartedness of employers and the greed
of unchecked competition."

Two systems are here contrasted: the System of Ownership and the
Wage System. These two systems may be set down systematically thus:

Wage System.	*Ownership System.*
1. The Wage System supposes a wage paid by an employer.	1. The Ownership System supposes a thing owned by an owner.
2. An employer employs an employee.	2. An Owner owns a thing owned.
3. An employer is a human being. An employee is a human being.	3. An owner is a human being. A thing owned is not a human being.
4. The essential relation of an employer is to a human being, i.e., the employee.	4. The essential relation of an owner is to a thing, i.e., the thing owned.
5. The employer as such is an owner. The employee as such is not an owner.	5. The owner as such is not an employer. The owner as such is not an employee.
6. The employer as such pays a wage to his employee. The employee as such receives a wage from his employer.	6. The owner as such uses a thing owned. The owner as such can sell a thing owned.

Wage System.	*Ownership System.*
7. Since employees as such are not owners, the more employees there are the fewer owners there are.	7. As an owner as such is not an employee (or employer), the more owners there are the fewer employees (and employers) there are.
8. The system in which there are many employees but few owners (and few employers) is called the Wage System.	8. The system in which there are many owners but few employees (and few employers) is called the Ownership System.
9. The more the Wage System increases the more the Ownership System decreases.	9. The more the Ownership System increases the more the Wage System decreases.
10. Any Law or Policy tending to increase the Wage System will tend to decrease the Ownership System.	10. Any Law or Policy tending to increase the Ownership System will tend to decrease the Wage System.

From all this we may gather the meaning and weight of the words of the *Rerum Novarum:* "Not only the legislative enactments (i.e., the Law) but the administrative action (i.e., the Policy) should tend to spread the system of ownership to as many as possible."

In saying "as many as possible" the *Rerum Novarum* does not venture to decide how far it is possible to make the humbler classes owners of their property in consumptive or productive goods. Thus it may, or may not, be possible for all workers, or all workers who are heads of families, to be owners. Or, again, it may be possible for all working heads of families to be mainly owners and partly wage-earners. Thus it is not at once evident how there could be a state of things in which there were no persons receiving wages for services rendered.

Yet it is the doctrine of the *Rerum Novarum* that the Law and Policy of nations should be to increase the number of owners and thereby to decrease the number of wage-earners.

The laws and administrative action needed to bring about this extension of the Ownership System and this diminution of the Wage System are for Legislatures and State departments to consider. For us, Catholics, the Distributive State (i.e., the State in which there are as many owners as possible) is not something which we discuss, but something we have to propagate and institute. No advance in social thought or social action is possible if we are seeking to prove to ourselves as a theory what we should be trying to realize as a fact.

If the wise and fruitful words of the *Rerum Novarum* needed any confirmation of their own clear implications, it would be found in the recent pronouncement of the Hierarchy of the United States:

> "Nevertheless, the full possibilities of increased production will not be realized so long as the majority of the workers remain mere wage-earners.
> The majority must somehow become owners."[58]

This pronouncement of the United States Hierarchy, with its peremptory MUST, we take to be a most decisive official utterance. We know of no commentary on this matter of the *Rerum Novarum* that carries the same official weight. This and the kindred pronouncement that where the Wage System obtains the Living Wage is "the first moral charge upon industry,"[59] make the words of these America Bishops one of the most important events of the century.

Do It Ourselves

WE WERE TALKING about the present breakdown of social machinery. It was agreed by both of us that when the King's Speech, or in other words the Government, of a few years ago confessed that unemployment could not be remedied by legislation, the breakdown of legislation was humbly admitted by the legislators. Moreover, it was agreed that a revolution, even if possible, was not politic. It would, as a matter of fact, heighten the evils it sought to destroy.

My friend began to feel depressed at this ultimate of thought as if the only alternatives before the people of England were the devil or the deep sea – slavery or the storm-havoc of revolution.

I said sharply, "We must do something."

To this he replied, almost with a snarl, "Yes, take the last shilling of last week's dole and hang ourselves."

I could not help saying: "That is a Eugenic reply." But I kept my bow on the harbour light by adding at once: "We can do for industrial freedom what Hungary and Ireland did for political freedom. Surely what they did for the lesser we can do for the greater."

My bullet found its billet. He almost leaped from his seat as he asked: "Have you a vision?"

"Every man has or may have a vision," I added, with a chill on my words, to keep him thinking. "It is not the vision that fails men; it is men who fail the vision. Facts and common sense are vision enough, Heaven knows, to make Utopia of Whitechapel.[60] But we men who dwell in Whitechapel do not dwell, as by desire we might dwell, in Utopia. We lie sick of a fever, trusting for a return to health to a prescription and a row of medicine bottles; whereas our lost health will come back to us only when we get up, get out, and get on with work for the wife and children in God's fresh air."

I could see that I must leave general principles to get to concrete facts or my friend would grind his teeth to toothache. I said: "Only a day or two ago you told me that the country is now giving some hundreds of thousands of pounds as a dole to the building trades. Yet if the house-builders need work, the workers need houses. Why, then, cannot *we* do something? The country has enough eyesight to see that it is not business to give as a dole for not working what could be given as a wage for work done."

"Yes," he added, "two and two make four. Much good that does."

I took his interruption with a smile. "The addition table is as holy as a creed. But it has to be lived. *Two and two make four* as a mere statement is the truth. But truth doesn't fill hungry mouths. You have to make, say, two potatoes into twenty-two potatoes by planting them in your field. Or you must make two strands, the warp and the woof, into cloth for your back."

Light was dawning in the night of his despairing eyes. He said: "Get on with your vision. I may take a hand in the venture."

I took up where I had left off; seeing my vision now as a historical event. "You remember my reading you an account of Birmingham house famine. A daily paper had reported (1) there was a shortage of several thousands of houses; (2) that there were thousands of men out of work; (3) that on a plot of several acres of land there were bricks, mortar, sand, lime, wood, iron, and everything necessary for house building. All that was necessary was CAPITAL – i.e., a piece of paper with someone's name written on it."

His eyes were a note of interrogation.

I answered them: "Cannot we do it ourselves? All the sensible men and women who love England will thank God for our intelligence!"

"That's a lot to think about!" be blurted out.

"I have even more where that comes from," I said, smiling. For me, visions are as definite and concrete as John the Evangelist's *one-hundred-and-fifty-three fish*. There was a time when the Northumberland and Durham Miners' Unions were perhaps the richest and, as they thought themselves, the most powerful unions in the world. What they did with their funds I don't know. They probably used them in ways which were a practical denial of the principles they were advocating. Perhaps they even lodged their funds with the bankers at 3½ per cent., who very kindly lent it back to the colliery company at 6 per cent. However, these most powerful unions might easily have bought a thousand or five thousand acres of real wealth in Northumberland as Lord Armstrong[61] did. Now if these unions had let this out in small holdings they would probably have doubled or trebled even its market value. I know a farm of five hundred acres, broken into small holdings, which is now worth five times its original value.

"If the unions had been wise they would have begun to organize themselves on a basis of self-support. Coalminers, I didn't tell you, can't eat coal. Neither will their stomach digest Bradburys. Napoleon used to say: 'An army crawls on its stomach.' My advice to the union would have been to organize a granary where there would always be at least one year's supply of wheat. You see——."

My friend rose from his seat. "I see – we must do things ourselves. I must sleep on this."

I added, gravely: "But you must awake from sleep if you are to do it yourself. And you must suffer a fool gladly, for I have more to say."

The British Association and the Wage System

To estimate what the British Association[62] has recently said on the Wage System we need to remember the words of the *Rerum Novarum*:

> "The law should favour ownership and its policy should be to induce as many as possible of the humbler classes to become owners."

As an owner as such is not a wage-earner as such, this explicit desire of the *Rerum Novarum* that the ownership system shall increase is an implicit desire that the wage system shall decrease. In this country there is a small group of thinkers to whom this doctrine of the *Rerum Novarum* means the justification of their economic opinions. These men give the Pope's vision a name. They call it "the Distributive State."

Economic Anarchy

The Economic Section of the British Association, at its recent annual meeting at Edinburgh, was faced with the almost unprecedented economic anarchy of the empire, and indeed of the world. The diagnosis of the economic ailment was not lacking in accurate description. Mr. Austin Hopkinson,[63] M.P., was trenchant in his denunciation of "Whitleyism, which could only lead them into a morass, as it was based on a wrong conception." He went on to speak of the diminished production. "Costs were too high because those who produced the goods were still endeavouring to get very much more return for their services than the economic situation would allow." With regard to the living wage, he said that "there was not much hope for civilization while they had a supposition that progress came simply through fuller stomachs.... Unemployment was due to the fact that we endeavoured to maintain a higher standard of living than the economic situation could justify."

The Wages Question

Mr. A. A. Mitchell,[64] in a paper on "The Breakdown of the Minimum Wage," agreed with Mr. Hopkinson. He said: "We were coming near, or perhaps had reached, the point where the entire wealth of the country was insufficient to pay the wages that were demanded." As wages are not primary wealth, nor even secondary wealth, but merely token wealth, statements like those of Mr. Mitchell seem to be merely words without meaning: that is, intellectual tokens backed by no reality.

The emptiness of modern economic thinking was further betokened by Mr. Mitchell's following statement. "A wage based on a standard of living and not on the value or selling price of the product tended to unemployment or inefficiency." The rightness or wrongness of this economic principle should be judged by its unexpressed conclusions. Mr. Mitchell may have meant that therefore the system of wages based on a standard of living should be abolished. If that was his meaning, his statement was economic wisdom. But he seems to have meant, not that the wage system should be abolished, but that a wage system should not be based on a standard of living. We presume, therefore, that it should be based on a standard of dying! In other words, what we want for the cure of unemployment is not a living wage, but a killing wage. Of course we need not say that these are not the words, but they are the philosophy, when expressed in simple language, of this school of economics from whom Mr. Mitchell has besought economic wisdom.

Potatoes *v.* Wheat

Perhaps it was only an untoward coincidence that Lord Bledisloe[65] addressed the Agricultural Section of the Edinburgh meeting on the superiority of potatoes to wheat as the basis of Britain's food supply in time of war! But it is significant that *The Times* gave greater space in its columns to the potato proposals of Lord Bledisloe than to any of the papers on Einstein's Theory of Relativity. No doubt that if the standard of living could be brought down from a bread to a potato basis, the country might see an increase in production.

An International Stable Standard of Value

Something like an attempt to trace economic evils to their economic causes was the main interest of a valuable statement which Professor Kirkaldy[66] contributed to a discussion "on an international stable standard of value." Professor Kirkcaldy "thought the present position was most remarkable. The raw materials which the world was crying out for existed in large quantities; the equipments for manufacturing the goods were greater than ever and abundant labour was waiting to be employed. All that was wanting was some medium of exchange to get the thing working."

We venture to suggest that in this very accurate diagnosis of the economic disease and its economic causes may be found one of the most incredible phenomena of all time. It is reminiscent of nothing so much as of a shell-shocked invalid who, having the physical and muscular power of walking or talking, lacks some other mysterious power or resolution to walk or talk. Again, it is reminiscent of the headstrong child who, on being asked to say "grateful," replied again and again, "But I can't say grateful!"

It is almost incredible that with the real wealth of labour and raw materials in abundance these two cannot be brought together for the increase of real wealth because of the breakdown of mere token wealth, to wit, gold, paper, or some other medium of exchange.

A Lesson in Economics

We cannot sufficiently repeat into the ears of the modern economic world that this token wealth, which today, by its aphasia, is preventing the junction of labour and raw material, is, ultimately a human will.

We are, then, faced with something like an economic principle applicable to all forms of money-organized industrialism. The principle may be formulated thus: "In the industrial organization of society the more physical friction decreases the more psychological friction increases." The present is not the occasion for proving this principle in the concrete. But we feel sure that to the operation of this principle is due the fact that machine production, which should by mathematical demonstration have given us quantitative plenty, has given us quantitative penury in the sphere of primary wealth.

Indeed, it would almost seem to be a psychological, if not an economic, ultimate that a system which was characterized by its expert knowledge and manipulation of token wealth would tend to give us more and more of this token wealth and less and less of real wealth.

The Unemployment Question

It must be repeated untiringly that there is no economic problem or evil of unemployment as such. The unemployment of the rich is looked upon even by our writers of fiction as one of life's boons. Moreover, the so-called unemployed are not really suffering from unemployment. They are for the most part employed, not in doing nothing, but in making nothing. They are busy going here and there looking for work; at a time when the land is going to ruin looking for workers!

The economic evil, therefore, is not the unemployment of the unemployed. It is the poverty of the unemployed. It is the lack of things of primary wealth, of food, clothing, housing, that makes the present epidemic of after-war unemployment one of the greatest tragedies of modern times. And this tragedy is now proving itself to be a justification of Pope Leo XIII's prophetic preference of a system of Ownership to a Wage System.

The Wage System Dying

We are witnessing, at least in this country, the wage system on its death-bed. Now death, even when it occurs most timely, is not without pains and dismay for those who witness and are benefited by its operation. Few of us can contemplate the change from a system we have lived under from childhood without thinking that something in the very nature of things is passing to nought. Yet if the wage system which alone these Edinburgh economists can envisage passes into an ownership system under the blessing of the Sovereign Pontiff we shall have the duty of remembering his wise word:

"A further consequence will result in the greater abundance of the fruits of the earth. Men always work harder and more readily when they work on what belongs to them.... That such a spirit of willing labour would add to the produce of the earth and to the wealth of the community is self-evident."

We recommend these wise words to next year's meeting of the British Association, if for no other reason than that they may not discuss the advisability of curing a world-wide disease by still larger draughts of the toxin poisoning from which the disease has sprung.

The Incubus of Industrialism

M R. LLOYD GEORGE, in moving to ask leave to introduce a Bill constituting a "Commission to inquire into the position of and conditions prevailing in the coal industry," said:

"Coal fetches food – (hear, hear) – coal pays for food. Coal pays the outgoing charges of a ship which comes back with food. What is the result? Half of the bread freights are paid by coal. If we destroy that export trade in coal, food goes up inevitably. You have got to send your ships in ballast to fetch it. Raw material goes up. I know of nothing more dangerous to a country like this, that must, whatever you do, depend for its raw material, and largely for its food, upon foreign lands."

To the ordinary citizen, and perhaps even to the ordinary member of Parliament, these grave words of the Prime Minister would seem weighty, if not conclusive. As we venture to doubt either their weight or their conclusiveness, we will try to put our readers at the point where they appear fallacious.

The Prime Minister's Contention

1. The Prime Minister's argument against the miners proposal of less work, more pay, and better conditions may be stated thus:

(a) Your proposals would mean that coal would go up 8s. or 10s. a ton.

(b) If coal goes up 8s. or 10s. a ton our export trade, especially in coal, will be ruined.

(c) If our export trade in coal is ruined we shall not be able to import food.

(d) If we do not import food we shall starve; because we cannot raise our own food.

2. It will easily be seen how questionable is every one of these four propositions. The Prime Minister, instructed, no doubt, by the coal owners experts, assumes that every rise in wages and shortening of hours would necessarily mean a rise in the price of coal. But the *Catholic Times*[67] rightly questioned this by suggesting that the Royal Commission now sitting should let us know "the exact cost of raising a ton of coal from the average mine, and the different charges subsequently incurred in conveying it to the consumer." Moreover, it suggested that there was something that should be met more seriously than by a gibe of Bolshevism in the miners contention that it is practicable to accept their proposals for less work, more pay, and better conditions without raising the price of coal to the consumer.

3. Moreover, the propositions (b) and (c) are highly uncertain to those who know the economic status of this nation. Moreover, some of our soundest economists view with unconcern the almost entire loss of our export and import trade; remembering the fact that the fate of Tyre and Sidon has lessons for all time.

Food Supplies

4. But the incubus of Industrialism is felt most in the proposition, "If we do not import food we shall starve; because we cannot raise our own food."

It would baffle the ordinary thinker on economic problems to set down the disputable propositions contained in this one statement.

The most important of these disputable propositions is that these islands cannot raise sufficient food for themselves. Our readers are now too well acquainted with the marvels of war farming to take this gloomy view of the fertility of our land or the intelligence of our land-workers.

5. But there is just one justification in Mr. Lloyd George's statement that he "knew of nothing more dangerous to a country like this, that must, whatever you do, depend for its raw material and largely for its food upon foreign lands." The phrase, "a country like this," saved the statement from being sheer untruth. It will be granted that while the country remains like this, it must depend largely upon foreign countries for its food. In other words, even in a country which probably yields the

necessaries of life more abundantly than any other country in the world, if much of the arable land is out of cultivation and many of the workers, instead of being on the land, are in factories and mines, then we grant that a country like this must depend for its food largely on foreign countries.

The Crowding of Factories and Mines

6. Industrialism, with its inhuman factories and mines, can do nothing to unmake the Britain it has made. Having taken the plough-man from the furrow, and still more the yeoman from his homestead, industrialism must be content that other countries with greater wisdom, if not intelligence, send their people out to the joyous toil of the wheat field and the vineyard whilst our people are condemned to the slavery of the coal mine and the cotton factory.

7. We have spoken of the incubus of Industrialism whilst thus dealing with the Prime Minister's speech because we find in that speech no higher vision than that of feeding the cancer which is gnawing into our national life. If the country with its wealth of mines – and its still greater wealth of food-growing lands – is to be organized for exports, then the efficient factory and the efficient mine will be the first necessity of national life. Moreover, in order to dispose of our exports we shall need a place in the sun, foreign markets, an efficient fleet, and the rest. Meanwhile our furrows will be deserted and our cradles empty. A people capable of freedom and of a noble life in their own homesteads will be crowded into the factory and the mine; where, deceived by loud praises of their freedom and their dignity, they will forget that they are the bondsmen not only of their paymasters at home, but of their freer, happier paymasters abroad.

Looking Towards the East

An Hour With A Northumbrian Seer

I FOUND HIM sitting on a grassy bank that looked eastward across the sea towards Lindisfarne.[68] It was August Bank Holiday. To judge by the sun, it was two hours before that splendid Royalty mounted his midday throne.

A book was in his hands. As I drew near him I had heard him declaim passages of it, with a slow cadence not unlike a psalm-tone of plain-song. "Anything may be expected of him," I said to myself as I drew near, "for has he not left a Tyneside ship-works and given up a manager's position worth £3,000 a year to come out on the land – or, as he calls it, 'my beloved North-Humber-Land'?"

His eyes alone gave token that he heeded my sitting down at his side. No rein was laid on his plainsong reading, which with its distinct metallic ring, seemed the contrast and complement of the velvet murmur made by the east wind in the hawthorn leaves behind our backs. He was reading, with a mist of tears in his flashing eyes, the great *Oratio Jeremiae* – the prayer of Jeremias the Prophet.

Suddenly he reined in his reading. He turned to the gurgling burn that tore its jagged way through a maze of underwood, and said dramatically:

> We have drunk our water for money,
> We have bought our wood. (Lam. v 4.)

I knew him so well in his moods of impersonal anger that I stood unquelled before the fierce inquisition of his eyes and the dagger-thrusts of his speech.

Modern Efficiency!

As I listened to him I seemed to hear a Greater than he calling His Father's Home of Prayer a "Den of Thieves." He said: "Modern efficiency! Come, let us adore thee – and fall down before thee – and worship thee. Modern Efficiency – the fiend."

His method of thinking was always so intuitive and elemental that I knew how to expect torn shreds, rather than a smoothly-woven web of thought. He went on: "The hell-fiend promised Jesus our Saviour all the power and glory of the world if only He would serve him – that is, if Truth would only serve a lie. But the ruse was worthy of the father of lies; for the power and glory even of the world are not the devil's – but God's – to give! A hundred years ago or thereabouts your machine-devil promised England and my beloved land north of the Humber that if only they would adore him they should be a land flowing with milk and honey. We believed the fiend because he may even have believed himself; until now we are a land, not flowing with milk and honey, but overflowing with margarine, crate-eggs, kept-fish, sterilized milk, anonymous jam, vermin-haunted flats made palatable by daintily-upholstered cinemas, non-stop tubes and listening-in!"—(An intended pause that seemed to throb like a startled pulse.)

"Listen to a priest who refused to sell his soul to hell. 'We have drunk our water for money, We have bought our wood.' This priest of God sees clearly, in the almost beatific vision of the eternal ideas, the hue of death where most men see the flush of life. He prophesies tomorrow because he has seen a thousand yesterdays. A civilization which herds its masses away from the wood and the brook, a people that pays so much a unit for water and buys kindle-wood at a price, has given up its sword to the enemy. Capitulation is only a matter of time. Death may be delayed, but cannot be withstood."

Babylon!

I saw him rapidly turn back the pages of his book, until he came to a passage which he solemnly and, if I may so say, liturgically kissed. Then, with a minor cadence and a semblance of thunder in his voice, he read: "Babylon is suddenly fallen, and destroyed! Howl for her! Take balm for her pain if so be she may be healed.

"We would have cured Babylon, but she is not healed. Let us forsake her and let us go every man to his own land" (Jer. li 9). He read out the last lines twice, his voice gradually rising, until it sounded like the loud evening cry of the bittern on the wild Northumbrian coast.

"Who but a priest – and what other people but the little chosen people of God – could thus have spoken to the great super-nation of Babylon? Only God could have given this priest of the little exiled people the sublime self-consciousness of the truth. He is not of the Imperial Race. He threatens it. He threatens to leave it. He foretells its fall. He bids his people quit the Machine before it crashes to its ruin.

"O song and prayer of an unsold prophet-priest! This strong cry to the God of his fathers he makes not only at the price of water and kindle-wood, and houses and...

"The neck-yoke of slavery;

but he weeps that the ancients have ceased from the gates (Parliament is bankrupt), the young men from the choir of the singers (God's sung praise is to seek), the joy of our heart is ceased, our dancing into mourning (and in our heart of hearts no joy is). Gone is wisdom from the gates – song from the sanctuary – joy from the heart – dance from the feet. And we are asked to be content with business governments and listening-in and – and race-suicide and jazzy fox-trots in overcrowded and super-heated rooms.

"Ugh! We on the land are told to be of good heart because, forsooth, we shall have telephone-poles, even in the two-acre plot of the land-worker. God help us. Are we not wise enough to know that as Roman roads meant the slavery of the lands they covered, so these town-made and town-controlled wire-poles will make the people on the land still more the slaves of the people in the town?

"Our great-grandparents, with a fine instinct for freedom, tried to break the machines, which in the end broke them. I sometimes wish their great-grandchildren amongst the land-workers would pull up the telephone poles, lest even our souls become enslaved.

"There is now no place for freedom or its godchild, originality, except somewhere in the depths of a desert or a forest. Yet deserts are rapidly being 'opened up' by tar-macadam roads, and forests are being wood-pulped to supply paper for our modern University, the Daily Press. *Heu mihi!*"

He rose up, and having walked rapidly to the water's edge, he stood looking towards the Holy Island muttering: "*Sancte Aidane, ora pro nobis. Sancte Cuthberte, ora pro nobis.*"

The Modern Town and Birth Control

UNTIL QUITE RECENTLY the working classes were so undeniably free from race-suicide that they were looked upon as a menace to the "better classes." Indeed the determined race-suicidal tendencies of the professional and moneyed classes were producing such a shortage of offspring everywhere except among the working population, that medical men and politicians were urging these professional and moneyed classes to practise conjugal chastity if only in self-defence. To none of these men was it a reassuring thought that, if statistics were to be trusted, the bloody Revolution effected by the guillotine was not as effective as would be the peaceful revolution of a people trained to the chastity of wedded parenthood.

If this point needed proof we should find it in a recent address given by Dr. C. K. Millard,[69] Medical Officer of Health for Leicester. This address was given on April 19th to the Leicester Rotary Club,[70] a society of business men. Our readers may need reminding that Dr. Millard has been so outspoken in his propagation of race-suicide as to be looked upon and called one of the foremost authorities in the country. He said:

> "With the establishment of permanent peace in Europe, there was no need to clamour for an increased birth-rate; rather we should welcome the declining birth-rate. Without doubt, a high rate of increase of population in any part of the world was only too apt to be associated with international aggressiveness.... Again, he might remind them as business men that a higher rate amongst the poorer classes undoubtedly meant higher taxes.... Moreover, a high birth-rate amongst the poorer grades of workers was certainly conducive to industrial unrest."†

Were we concerned to refute this Neo-Malthusian Medical Officer of Health, we would point out the fact that he brings forward not medical, but economic arguments!

---

† *Leicester Daily Post*, April 20

But for the moment the significant fact is not that a Medical Officer justifies to a club of rich men his stench of Neo-Malthusianism by bad economics, but that his arguments and his Neo-Malthusianism are proving acceptable to the working men.

What the West End Took Eastwards

Gradually the venereal leprosy has crept eastward from the West End. When slumming became the fashion we used to hear, even in Catholic circles, how good it was that West went East "to help the poor working people in their struggles," etc. West has gone East, bringing gifts; foremost of which is the stench and filth of race-suicide. All students of sociology know that amongst the working classes this crime was almost unknown until it was deliberately taught by those who lay under the terror of the survival of the socially unfit. Even though the success of this propaganda has been phenomenal, it has not yet satisfied the economic appetite of such Borough Medical Officers of Health as Dr. Millard or the Eugenic appetite of Sir George Newman,[71] the Chief Medical Officer of the Ministry of Health!

Bad Housing

But this apostolate of race-suicide which the well-to-do classes have so successfully propagated amongst the honest work-people would have had few chances of success if the work-people had not been driven into straits where race-suicide seemed almost inevitable. Modern industrialism, now hardly more than one hundred and fifty years old, has outlived its promises to the working people. It promised them not indeed the best (because it humbly acknowledged that only hand-craft could give them the best of anything), but more of the second and third beat. Even these modest promises it has now belied; and perhaps forgotten. At any rate, whilst there is no end of things which were not known in the "dark ages" of Moses, Plato, Phidias,[72] Augustine,[73] Aquinas, Shakespeare – in other words, whilst there is no end of railways, telegraphs, telephones, typewriters, aeroplanes, motor-cars, cinemas and such like, England, one of the richest countries in the world, has a shortage of a million houses! In some of our great cities, where hundreds of millions of money are yearly made by manufacturers, landlords are making money by letting, not merely rooms, but landings.

The Temptations of Industrial Centres

These are facts which make working people look upon race-suicide as the "shortest way out." Their paymasters of yesterday told them they should not have large families; because they and the State could not afford them. Today, when they have forgotten from whose lips they yesterday heard the refrain, the men and women of London, Birmingham, Manchester, Glasgow, and other industrial centres are following in the sinful ways of their masters and paymasters, on the plea which, God knows, seems reasonable enough, that there is no room or food for a large family in the modern large town.

The Clergy and the People

As a priest, then, I seem to realize, when perhaps it is too late, that Industrialism has won, and will remain the victor until a second Moses leads the people from the brickyards and organised slavery of our modern Egypts. No campaign in favour of the large family and against the empty cradle is likely to be effective whilst married couples, even in mining towns, can scarcely find a house, where many families are housed in two rooms, and some human beings have no home but a landing. To urge these people to have a large family seems cruel enough to deserve the anger of St James: "If a brother or sister be naked and want daily food, and one of you say to them, Go in peace, be you warmed and filled; yet give them not those things that are necessary for the body, what shall it profit?"† † Jas. ii 15,16

We priests of God must help our people to keep the law of God concerning wedlock and begetting by helping them to end those conditions of servile industrialism which make it almost a matter of heroic virtue to live in the spirit of the psalmist:

> Thy wife as a fruitful vine on the sides of thy house,
> Thy children as olive branches round about thy table.

(Ps. 127.)

Nazareth Measures

An Open Letter to the Next Prime Minister

A S YOUR IDENTITY is still, while I write, unknown both to yourself and to me, I shall have no misgivings about the pain my words may give. It is not as a politician, but as a priest, I offer you some of the official wisdom learned from my masters. In other words, I humbly offer you in your day of power the gathered wisdom of a class, who, whilst holding aloof from the politics of the City of Man, have yet given their blessing and counsel to every historic city men have built.

If your will is even level with your power you may be able to add a few courses in the building up of the England that is to be. Yet, unless your eyes have hitherto been held, you will have learned that stone upon a stone does not make a wall; nor wall joined to wall, a city.

The Builder

more than any other craftsman, needs the level, the plummet, the square. Every stone he sets must be in its place under pain of endangering even the stones already set. He who would raise a city, a house, or even a wall, must be humble enough to true the work of his hand ten thousand times in the working.

Here may I call your mind from Whitehall to Greenwich – from the business of Whitehall to the significance of Greenwich? At Whitehall there is a throng of men, legislators and administrators, and a still denser throng of clerks to the legislators and administrators. All these men are engaged in scanning England, and Englishmen.

At Greenwich there is a small group of men who scan the stars!

Yet without Greenwich what and where would Whitehall be? The ship of the State would be without helm or chart if Whitehall alone were the guide. But the little group of men who scan the skies, and keep...

A Thousand Vigils

in their love of the stars are the seers without whose wisdom the ship of the State would be helpless in the trough of the seas. Few men are given gold for their services more stintedly than these scholars whose eyelids are "gold-dusty" through living with the stars. Yet if gold were the authentic reward of service these men would be the millionaires of our modern civilization. It is not you of Whitehall, of even you, the *Collegium Pontificum* of Downing Street, who control. It is these "starry amorists," whose star-standards of length and weight and heat and force and time measure the very garments we wear and the hours at which our legislators foregather to deliberate.

*****

From Greenwich learn the significance of Nazareth. Jerusalem was a Metropolis as London is a Metropolis. Nazareth was a village as, compared with London, Greenwich is a village. But Nazareth, like Greenwich, is the place where all the Sovereign Measures are verified and kept.

Greenwich Time

measures our day. Nazareth Time is the measure even of eternity. All our personal and social building, to be lasting, must be trued by the measures of that little school of Seers whose names are the very music of life – Jesus, Mary, Joseph!

Most humbly, then, do I beseech your wisdom, if not your power, to pilgrim ever and anon to Nazareth lest you be found to have builded in vain. The time measure of Nazareth is nothing less than Eternity; and the Master of the Measures none other than the Ancient of Days. Therefore in all your law-making be what Plato wished all men, and especially all lawmakers, to be: "spectators of all time and all existence." The Home of Nazareth recalls our poet's words: "They dreamed not of a perishable home who thus could build" Moreover, the...

Nazareth Measure

of length and weight and worth is the Family – that terrestrial "Holy and Undivided Three." Let no guile of social usefulness betray you into hurting the authority of the Father, the chastity of the Mother, the rights and therefore the property of the Child. Social and economic laws are more subtle but not less infallible than physical law. No programme of good intentions will undo the mischief caused by an interference with family life. As well try to arrest a thrown bomb by a plea of good intentions as try to prevent the final ruin of the State by the plea that our ruin of the family was well intentioned. Give no heed to the buyers and sellers who would make Whitehall seek its ultimate measures from Lombard Street and not from Greenwich. England's final doom is not with the trader and his wares, but with the Seer and his stars. And Nazareth, not Jerusalem, is the City of the Measures of God's kingdom on earth.

Nature and Unemployment

THE COLUMNS OF THE PRESS have been filled of late with two discussions on "Back to the Land" and "Unemployment." Most of the disputants have shown such deep interest in the subject as to be largely irritable with any scheme but one of their own making. To some of us the two discussions are not really two, but one. The epidemic of unemployment, now so recurrent in this country, is as certainly connected with the land as hay is connected with grass. To put the matter sententiously – The question of unemployment is the question of the land.

The People and the Soil

1. On November 19, 1920, the Prime Minister spoke in the House of Commons on the Agriculture Bill. Few words of his have been truer or more unheeded. He said:

> This country was a little top-heavy in many respects. The percentage of people based on the soil was small. He had many times discussed the subject with foreign Ministers, and they had said: "This or that country is safe, for the bulk of the people are on the land." A safe country was a country where there was a large percentage of population engaged in the calmest and steadiest of all industries. It was in the interests of the people, not only its security against foreign peril, but in the interests of the security of society itself, that we should have a larger percentage of population engaged in the cultivation of the soil.

Agriculture and the Unemployed

2. This stability and security achieved by agriculture is nowhere more manifest than in the unique power of agriculture to deal with unem-

ployment. Last year at Cardiff the president of the Economic section of the British Association, Dr. J. H. Clapham,[74] formulated this truth as a plain historic fact. He contrasted the year 1920 with the year 1820; the Great War in which England and France had been victorious against Germany with the great war in which England and Germany had been victorious against France. "Demobilization in France presented few of the problems familiar to us. Probably not one man in ten demobilized was a pure wage-earner. The rest had had links with the soil. The land neglected during the war was crying out for labour.... Things were different in England.... Three hundred thousand soldiers and sailors had been discharged. They were simply thrown on the labour market; and the vast majority of them were wage-earners.... Great Britain alone was partially industrialized in 1815–1820; and Great Britain, though victorious, suffered acutely."

Hand-Work and Machinery

3. It is in the nature of things that agriculture should outdistance machine-industrialism in dealing with unemployment. A machine-filled factory cannot easily adapt itself to sudden fluctuations in the number of its hands. If there are few hands the machinery is at a standstill; if there are too many hands the hands themselves are at a standstill. A machine, as such, can work only a definite twenty-four hours a day, and can be served by only a definite number of hands. But the land can meet fluctuation in the number of land workers with equanimity. It loses little of its riches if through lack of workers it is forced into fallow. It only gains in riches if the number of workers is increased. Indeed, nowhere does the law of diminishing returns come into operation so late. There is almost no end to the increased returns yielded to increased cultivation. When machine labour gives place to hand labour and foot labour, as in market gardens, the land comes into its own. The saturation-point of labour is at a higher altitude in land-work than in any other form of human toil.

England's Untilled Land

4. But in this country we are far from saturation point. The untilled land of England – probably the richest in Europe – is crying out, not

against more labour, but for more labour. It is calculated that at present there are some 2,000,000 unemployed. But the Prime Minister, in his speech on the Agriculture Bill, said that "there had been a decrease of something like 3,000,000 in those working on the land!" The coincidence of the two totals is almost of the nature of a doom fulfilled!

5. Moreover, during the time of unemployment the land shows its superiority. Unemployment in an industrialized community means that many men are engaged in producing little or nothing, and in consuming much. It would be instructive to have accurate statistics of the work-hours lost to the nation by the present wave of unemployment, which all accredited economists foresaw and foretold with scientific accuracy. But even during the rare periods of unemployment which visit a well-ordered agricultural community there is no day when the workers may not do work which is the production, however slender, of real wealth.

The New Industrial Charter

To EVERY CATHOLIC who is anxious to end or mend the social ills few words of Pope Leo XIII's *Rerum Novarum* are more significant than those in which he outlines the not impossible Utopia of a "Distributive State":

> The law therefore should favour ownership; and its policy should be to induce as many as possible of the humbler classes to become owners. Many excellent results will follow.
>
> ...First of all, property will certainly become more equitably divided.
>
> ...If the working people can be encouraged to obtain a share in the land...the gulf between vast wealth and sheer poverty will be bridged.
>
> ...A further consequence will result in the greater abundance of the fruits of the earth....
>
> ...A third advantage...men would cling to the country in which they were born.

In contrast with these words, which are a real Workman's Charter, stands the "Report of the Provisional Joint Committee appointed by the Industrial Conference."[75] This Report is now complete. To those who have heard the Papal Charter this so-called "New Industrial Charter" makes pitiful reading.

The Terms of Reference

Not that we were expecting from the framers of the Report a document of any other spirit than the Report they have issued. It was plain that a Report substantially different was not included within their commission. The terms of reference to the Provisional Joint Committee responsible for the Report were as follow:

To consider and report to a further meeting of the Conference
on the causes of the present unrest, and the steps necessary to safeguard and promote the best interests of employers and work-people
(sic) and the State, and especially to consider:

1. The questions relating to hours, wages, and general conditions of employment;

2. Unemployment and its prevention;

3. The best methods of promoting co-operation between capital and labour.

It is clear that in these terms of reference is contained an ideal
widely apart from the ideal of the *Rerum Novarum*. The Papal Encyclical
lays upon States the duty of favouring ownership (*"Favere huic juri leges
debent"*); so that as many as possible of the humbler classes shall become
owners. Now as an owner, as such, is neither an employer nor an employee,
but a worker, the more owners there are the fewer employers and employees will there be. In other words, the *Rerum Novarum* lays upon States the
duty of passing laws which will tend to decrease the number of employers
and employees by increasing the number of owners.

The Committee Restricted

But the Provisional Joint Committee of the Industrial Conference
were not empowered even to consider the advisability of such a state of
things. By their terms of reference they could consider only what would
"promote the best interests of employers and work-people" (i.e., employees), "and especially the best methods of promoting co-operation between
capital and labour." It was therefore altogether beyond their terms of
reference to consider the best methods of promoting not co-operation
between capital and labour, but the identification of capital and labour.
Thus the Papal Charter seeks to bring about a state of things in which
there will be the greatest number of owners and consequently the least
number of wage-earners; in other words, the *Rerum Novarum* seeks not
to perpetuate the wage system, but, as far as possible, to substitute for the
wage system a system of ownership.

On the other hand, the Joint Committee by their terms of reference
could consider only the perfecting and therefore the perpetuation of the
wage system.

The Wage System

If this contrast between the ideals of the Papal Charter and the so-called "New Industrial Charter" is valid, the latter becomes very painful reading. We are told that the Joint Committee responsible for the Report consisted of thirty representatives of the employers and thirty representatives of trade unions. We are also told, what we could not otherwise have believed, that the Report is unanimous, and that it is signed by the chairman, Sir Allan Smith,[76] Chairman of the employers representatives, and Mr. Arthur Henderson,[77] Chairman of the trade union representatives.

So fully accepted is the employee and wage ideal rather than the owner and ownership ideal that we have hardly the heart to point out the danger to personal freedom lurking in some of its provisions. Thus we have the principle of a National Industrial Council and the other apparatus of the Whitley Report.[78] Again, we read: "The basis of negotiation between employers and work-people should be a full and frank acceptance of employers organizations and trade unions as the recognized organizations to speak and act on behalf of their members. Members should accept the jurisdiction of their respective organizations." We do not say that this provision by its very nature will do away with the workers last weapon, the right to strike. But we would ask the workers if they have fully grasped the possibilities which lie beneath its innocent surface.

Cardinal Bourne's Warning

Workers should never forget the wise words of his Eminence the Cardinal-Archbishop[79]: "While the Constitution had increasingly taken on democratic forms, the reality underlying those forms had been increasingly plutocratic. Legislation under the guise of social reform tended to mark off all wage-earners" (note the word "wage-earners") "as a definitely servile class." These wise words of the Cardinal Archbishop should lead workers to be very cautious in accepting legislation under the guise of social reform, lest they be found to have been misled by outer democratic forms into accepting a plutocratic reality which marks them off still more definitely as a servile class.

A Grammar of Unemployment

FOR THE PURPOSE of clear economic discussion we still lack a definition of Unemployment. If it is defined as a state of work-lessness, this nominal definition throws us back on the difficult definition of work. We have but unveiled the difficulty by defining work as human effort acting on material substances for the needs of human life. Such a definition would make it possible to exclude priests and not to exclude professional thieves from the class of workers.

Though it is perhaps impossible to find thinkers agreed about "what is unemployment," there is almost a common agreement about "who are the unemployed." We do not rank the sick among the unemployed, because their human effort, though intense, is a patient acceptance of physical evil rather than an active transformation of material goods. Nor, tragically enough, do we rank among the employed the dispirited men who trudge mile after mile across our great cities, with blistered feet, in search of work; though assuredly they make human effort enough to supply human needs.

But we are agreed that at present there are more than a million men and women, at once capable and bereft of employment to such an extent that they cannot procure the needs of human life. No real contribution to the problem of unemployment can be made except by showing how unemployment may be cured. But, as we cannot suggest the real cure for unemployment without discovering its real cause, our Grammar of Unemployment becomes an attempt to diagnose the causes of unemployment.

The two variable elements in our provisional definition of unemployment are human effort (or activity) and material things. The element of human need is practically constant.

Unemployment may therefore be caused by a defect (a) of human effort, or (b) of material things.

This defect of human effort may be either (a) non-volitional – e.g., through physical defect, as in children, the sick, etc.; or through mental defect, as in the feeble-minded, etc. Or it may be (b) volitional. Volitional unemployment may be right, by springing from a good will, or it may be wrong by springing from an ill will. Thus, a man who is rightly taking a short or a prolonged rest is, so far, unemployed. This kind of right volitional unemployment presents no special problem to the economic thinker.

But the kind of wrong volitional unemployment is one of the greatest problems which the economic thinker is bound to face. Thus, a man may be unemployed because he will not work. He may be physically and mentally capable of the human effort which transforms material things for human needs. But he may be volitionally opposed to work. This class may be subdivided logically, psychologically, and perhaps historically into (1) those who do not wish to do any work and (2) those who do not wish to do this or that work. Few men are absolutely work-shy. But many men are relatively work-shy in their distaste for this or that kind of work. An example of this relative work-shyness is the indisposition of factory hands to become land workers Though land work is much more varied, healthy, interesting, and human than the normal occupation of a factory, yet the attractiveness of the towns, where factories flourish, unfits men for the realities of the land. It may perhaps be stated as a principle that where the great mass of the citizens are so relatively work-shy as to prefer work of secondary value to work of primary value, unemployment will be recurrent, and perhaps permanent instead of sporadic. Moreover, it will tend to be fatal.

National Factors

One of the gravest subjects of discussion at the present time is the influence of certain national factors in the production of this volitional work-shyness. Thus a moralist might enquire how far a national decay of belief in the divinity of Jesus Christ leads to unemployment as a recurrent national disease. Again, a political thinker might ask how far is our system of primary, secondary, and university education calculated to unfit men for dealing with the production of real wealth; how far it fits them only for the production of token wealth; and therefore how far it infallibly leads to volitional unemployment.

Our second cause of unemployment may be due not proximately to a defect of human effort, but to a defect of material things.

This defect of material things may be (a) non-volitional, or (b) volitional. (N.B.—We venture to suggest that in this, as in all economic questions, the chief factor is the human will.)

Importance of Transport

Non-volitional defect of material things may be due (1) either to a lack of things themselves, or (2) to a lack of the means of transporting them to where they are available for human effort. Thus the cotton-spinners of Lancashire would be thrown into unemployment if the cotton crop failed, or if the fleet of cotton-ships sank on their homeward trip. The mystery of the famine in Vienna has been attributed to the breakdown of railway transport from the local wheat lands which had hitherto supplied food for the clerical and operative millions of Vienna.

Volitional defect of material things is either (1) deliberate, or (2) indeliberate. Deliberate volitional defect of material things may be either for the explicit purpose of causing an economic margin of unemployment, or it may be for the explicit purpose of making more profits. The utilitarian doctrine that "a margin of unemployment is good for trade" has been credited with too many victories not to be still advocated as a national policy. Again, it is not always realized that greater profits can be made by producing as little as possible of a commodity and by selling as dearly as possible. In both these cases unemployment is a necessary result.

At present it is necessary to examine all schemes for dealing with unemployment, lest they may be found to afford relief to the present visible suffering only by increasing the present hidden disease.

Authority and Property

An Open Letter to the Prime Minister

YOUR UNEXPECTED RETURN to power can hardly fail to flood you with letters from friends and foes who wish either to float with you on the incoming tide or to withstand you to the face. If I ask you to single out this open letter from the deluge of friendly and hostile correspondence it is because the counsels it presumes to offer may be perhaps unique. It is more than likely that the letters you have received or will receive are of politicians to you, a politician. That will be their worth or worthlessness to you in your post of political responsibility. This letter, on the contrary, is from one who is not a politician, but an ethical practitioner. Indeed, it is from one who in order to keep his mind set on the ethical rather than on the political aspect of politics deliberately abstained from using his political vote. As his suffrage, though not cast for you, was not cast against you, he need not be taken for your enemy but as your friend, even though he seek to speak the truth.

In the first place, therefore, I beg of you to show your country the essential sanity of garnering wisdom from failure, and good from evil, Your long exile from political supremacy would indeed be lost if it had given you no insight into the woes and rights of a minority. Theories of the Divine Right of Sovereigns did not die with the Stuarts. They are still dominant with those who, whilst explicitly denying the Divine Right of Kings, are agreed that one of the first duties of a majority is reprisals; for that minorities most suffer.

In the next place, Sir, you will be all the more borne to rest your rule on ethical principles rather than arithmetical majorities when you realize that the majority you do in fact command is one of those eccentric phenomena due to our, perhaps, belated system of suffrage. Of the 14,000,000† voters whose political opinions were recorded by the use of

---

† Ten returns had not been received at the date of writing this letter.

the vote you polled 5,377,465; or some 38 per cent. Thus an electorate minority of 38 per cent. is in a position of supremacy over an electorate majority of 62 per cent.! In other words, 38 per cent. of the Parliamentary voters control 56 per cent. of the Parliamentary votes. We do not say that this is politically right or wrong; seeing that we are not uttering political opinions. But in reminding you of the fact that you represent only a minority of your countrymen we would ask you not to forget that the only divine right conceded alike to majorities or minorities is based upon the fulfilment of divine duties. Truth and justice are not decided by the suffrage of the Ballot Box!

Hints For a Programme

Again, if we are to believe the reported speeches of the candidates, you have not come into power by reason of any constructive programme; but almost in sheer weariness of a Coalition which was one of the temporary necessities of the chaos following upon war. Your sudden return to power may have made it impossible to find time for any programme of construction. May I then remind you of two explicit principles of your own party which might give you the right to serve your country and even to deserve its gratitude? Of these two principles the first is that of Authority and Obedience. The Conservative Party in whose fellowship you pride, have maintained, with what truth I judge not, that the principle of Authority and Obedience to Authority differentiates them from the Liberal party whose watchword has been "liberty." For the moment I need not urge the fact that these two principles, though seemingly so opposite, are at heart one.

Authority and Obedience

I would only suggest that the principle of Authority and Obedience, if duly carried out, might give you not a "catch-majority," but the solid suffrage of the people. But this principle must be not so much the authority of those who command and the obedience of those who are commanded; but the OBEDIENCE OF AUTHORITY. Disobedience is culpable in all classes It is most culpable and most dangerous in those who should command. No authority, given directly or indirectly by God, is essentially of any binding power unless it is itself in obedience to the divine rights, conferred by God on the lowliest of His human creatures. "Bad Laws are No Laws" is a maxim of St Thomas Aquinas, now sanctioned and promulgated by Pope Leo XIII (*Rerum Novarum*). If, then, you and your fellow-politicians who are for the moment in power can give England the example of an Authority which is less concerned to safeguard its own rights than to fulfil its own duties – in other words, if you as a fount of Authority can set a model of Obedience, the people whom you control will follow where you lead.

The Rights of Property

To this principle of Authority and Obedience add your second historic principle of the Rights of Property which is perhaps only the principle of Authority and Obedience applied to the external wealth of the citizens. If, even in economics, it is a more blessed thing "to give than to receive," surely you may see that the safeguarding of the most necessary property is the first call upon the energy of the party in power, and especially of a party fundamentally based on the rights of property. Remember, too, that no property is so sacred as the property of those who are always within the danger-zone of poverty.

To quote the authoritative words of Pope Leo XIII:

"Rights must be religiously respected wherever they exist.... It is for this reason that wage-earners who are undoubtedly among the weak and necessitous should be especially cared for and protected by Government." The sacred principle of Property is, therefore, most endangered not when a challenge is given to the "small number of very rich men who have been able to lay upon the teeming masses of the labouring poor a yoke little better than that of slavery itself"; but when no attempt is made to give back to these teeming masses the things that are theirs.

The historic Conservative Party might vouchsafe to England a much-needed example of self-sacrifice if these two fundamental principles of Authority and Property were carried out after the intention of their divine Author. But it has been said, with what truth I cannot and do not judge, that the historic Conservative Party has become a plutocracy.

If this statement is true, light is thrown on the solemn words of the After-War Pastoral of his Eminence Cardinal Bourne, which contains further statement well worthy of your thought:

> Capitalism began really with the robbery of Church property in the sixteenth century, which threw the economic and social advantage into the hands of the land-owning and trading classes. The Industrial Revolution of the eighteenth century found England already in the hands of the well-to-do classes. The effect of competition uncontrolled by morals has been to segregate more and more the Capitalist from the wage-earning classes, and to form the latter into a PROLETARIAT, a people owning nothing but their labour power and tending to shrink more and more from the responsibilities of both ownership and freedom.
>
> By the beginning of the twentieth century...the territorial oligarchy had thoroughly fused with the commercial magnates and the fusion had produced plutocracy. While the Constitution had increasingly taken on democratic forms, the reality underlying these forms had been increasingly plutocratic. Legislation under the guise of SOCIAL REFORM tended to mark off all wage-earners as a definitely servile class.†

If ever words of truth justified the juxtaposition of St Edward's and St Stephen's, Westminster, it is surely these plain words of a Cardinal Archbishop full of the spirit of Lanfranc[80] and à Beckett.[81] They would provide a fit subject for the deliberations of the first Cabinet which you summon; for they will provide England with the means of judging whether your tenure of power has been for the good or ill of England.

---

† *The Nation's Crisis*, by Cardinal Bourne.

The Arrival of a Fact

AYOUNG FATHER writes to his friend on the birth of his first-born:

It is now a week since I meant to make you a partner in my joy by telling you that God has been good enough to send me a little daughter. But the week has passed with a barrage of excitement and work, which has left me no time for the calls of friendship, and little or none even for food. The week you and I spent on the Vimy Ridge was a holiday compared to the crowded happenings of these last eight days. Indeed, I have to make an act of faith in the almanack in order to call it a week. By psychoanalysis it seems the best part of a month. This day week seems to be, not so much eight days ago as a civilization ago.

I have the extraordinary sensation of having been born again. By this I do not merely mean that the pains borne by Kate in her child-bearing were agony to me. We men are not fitted to see women suffer physical pain. It reminds us too much of vicarious suffering. It seems to recall us to our sins.

It is not this agony of sympathy that made and still makes me feel almost as young and wonderstruck as my little blue-eyed Mary (I forgot to say that her name is Mary – Queen Mary!). When I come to think of it, the cause of my feeling the pangs and joys of second birth is that new-born, first-born Mary of the blue eyes and clasped fingers is a fact, like the battle of Hastings or the Pyramids or Mount Everest. Now facts are not merely stubborn things; they are extraordinary subtle things. Venal lawyers and slattern philosophers glibly contrast law and fact, to the entire discredit of the latter. But when I came to reflect on the dimpled fact that I found nestling in Kate's arms, I suddenly saw how it takes a thousand laws to make even one fact.

A New World of Thought

Queen Mary, by no talk of hers, but by mere existence, an existence so frail that a breath could have quenched it, begot me into a new world of thought. Honestly, until my little daughter came I think I have never thought, Perhaps the best that could be said of me was that I tasted thinking, as wine-tasters turn a wine in their mouth without – ahem! – making it their own. But when I was allowed into the Birthroom, which I promptly called the Bethlehem Chamber, thoughts came so fast that I remembered your old paradox "We men are by nature not the gentler, but only the weaker sex." I could see at once that Kate, having been within hail of death, was no longer a girl, a woman, or even a wife, but a mother. Though she smiled at me as she had always smiled, she now turned her eyes and mine towards our "gift from God most high." In that common look towards the daughter of our wedded love, Kate and I knew that we had passed out of an old world in to a new. *Deo gratias.*

By her almost frightening delicacy our Mary was a stupendous fact. Kate and I felt instinctively that whilst we were giving something with conscious gladness to our little one, we were really insolvent bankrupts by what we were receiving from the unconscious largesse of our babe. When in the past few months we had our moments of misunderstanding made sensitive by our dose of common humanity each had found it hard to yield to the other.

The Dominant Factor of the Home

But now there was a third party to every misunderstanding. The little bundle of rights which had reached life only because its mother had risked death was now the dominant factor in every home trouble. This was the birth of a new thought within me. I could see the devilry of divorce as I had never seen it before. True, I had believed it on the word of the Church. God had now sent my little daughter as an authentic vision in which I could see what I had only believed. It was now as clear as Mary's blue eyes that the chief factor in divorce as such is not the rights and wrongs of the husband or wife, but the duties of the father and mother resting on the rights of the child. Suddenly, as my little daughter cried in her mother's arms, and my limbs seemed to become "ashes of tow" under me, I knew that a land is doomed to death if the marriage bond becomes practically the relationship of a husband and a wife to each other, and not the relationship of a father and mother to a child.

Parental Duties

That evening, on my way to my union, of which I am secretary, I kept saying: "The rights of man – bosh ! But the duties of a father! The rights of a father!" As a young man beginning to be a wage-earner, my hunger and thirst for justice had been but a masked brand of selfishness. When Kate became mine to work for, my unselfishness began to be challenged by a husband's duty of loving and cherishing his wife. But Mary, whom Kate and I had chosen to be our child, was or could be the end of all selfishness. As I passed through the mirk and mud of one of London's worst slums, my soul was born to the fact that on me lay the duty of giving my little daughter some fitter dowry of life than was now the lot of the majority of her brothers and sisters. I felt the need of a holy of holies in little – a home, a homestead, where the child who had brought Kate and me such gifts by her coming should have room and air to live and thrive as God would have her live and thrive.

A Glimpse of Heaven

Archimedes once said: "Give me a fulcrum and I will move the world." God having sent me a little daughter, the world I lived in hitherto has moved and I whom you used to call an earthworm for my love of earth have a glimpse of a kingdom into which I have been led by a little child. Now you know what I mean when I rock Queen Mary's cradle, saying: "Love unblessed of God was nigh the death of me. But Love, who art my God, Thou art the birth of me."

Rights of the Parent

IN THESE MOMENTS when the State, which only succeeds in "muddling through" its own task of civil government, is preparing to take over the still harder task of bringing up families, it is the duty of Catholics to realize the rights of parents.

1. The Rights of the Parent are Natural Rights. Our English language does not bring out the full force of the Latin words *natura, naturalis,* which are here used. It is almost a pity that we cannot literally translate the more accurate Latin by saying "The rights of the parent are *birth-rights.*" In saying that we mean that these rights are not *statutory* rights depending on man's will, but they are natural rights depending on man's nature (*natura,* or birth). By this we do not deny that these rights may come into existence in any individual case, and thus may be occasioned, by man's act. Thus marriage, which is the remote occasion, and procreation, which is the proximate occasion of these rights, are confessedly the acts of man. But according to the teaching of Catholic theologians these acts are obligatory on the human race, not indeed as individuals, but as a race.

The Will of God

When, therefore, a child is born its parents find themselves possessed of certain rights which, though occasioned by their own acts of marriage and procreation, are not determined by their own will, nor by the will of the State, nor by the will of man, but by the will of God.

2. The Rights of the Parent are prior to the Rights of the State. This is clearly seen by those who recognise the Catholic doctrine that the family as a family is prior to the State. Not only in idea but in fact, families must have preceded States. The primitive political organization

presupposes a group of primitive families. Indeed, the very idea which lies at the root of a State, and all the political arts which make States possible, are borrowed from the natural organization of the family. The wedded union of two hearts that beget a third is no gift or doing of the State's. It is older than any commonwealth. It would still live if all commonwealths came to death.

It is truer to say that the State has duties towards the family than that families have duties towards the State. A nation's chief duty towards this living and essential thing is to safeguard it. But they that watch over it must never sleep, and never overstrain their powers of defence. It is such a sacred thing, so delicately shapen and framed by God, that even its defenders must not lay thoughtless hands upon it lest, like the over-willing defenders of the Ark, they be struck dead.

Thus the home, with its dowry of natural rights, is an older institution than any law or Parliament of men.

A Great Principle

3. The Rights of the Parent are the Best Safeguard of the Rights of the Child. This principle is one which psychology guarantees as an idea and history witnesses to as a fact.

Thoughtless folk whose vision has been darkened by meddlesome philanthropy can hardly be expected to see that even in idea childhood could have no better guardian than parenthood. These people are often heard to ask "why we hear so much about the rights of parents, and so little about the rights of children." Their foolish question shows them ignorant of the psychological principle that although the rights of parent and child seem to be two, these two are really one. Until the child is of an age to defend itself against those who merely seek to use it, or improve it as a means to an end, the child's rights are centred in the parent, the only one whom nature has empowered to love it as an end in itself. No other institution in the world either loves the child as the parent loves it, or even loves it at all.

Indeed, far greater and more unselfish than the love which provides nine-tenths of the matter of our fiction is the love which is rarely dramatized. The romance of two souls who take themselves for better or worse is hardly more than a symbol for that extraordinary love which springs up between the parent and the child. Indeed, in the history of mankind the most marvellous deeds have been wrought by the bread-winner for his babe in his home, or by the mother for the suckling at her breast.

Parents' Love

It will be said that many parents are unfit for their task or even disloyal to their duties. Many, I agree, in the aggregate; but few in proportion to the millions of parents in the world. Indeed, the devoted love of even modern parents to their children is probably the vastest social force in the world. Although a violent crusade against parenthood has now been troubling humanity for a century, the devotion of parents as parents has no rival except the devotion of men and women as children of God.

Dangerous Legislation

For the thousandth time we must warn Catholics against benevolent legislation which seeks "the life of the child," only to accomplish its death. We do not accuse these legislators of being evil by design, because we do not know whether the evil they work is wrought by malice or ignorance. We only know that whereas malice is always the greater crime, ignorance may often be the greatest danger. Moreover, we are reminded of the never-to-be-forgotten words of his Eminence Cardinal Bourne: "Legislation under the guise of Social Reform tended to mark off all wage-earners as a definitely servile class. While the Constitution had increasingly taken on democratic forms, the reality underlying these forms had become increasingly plutocratic." It would ill become the Catholics of these countries to be found once more asleep; especially in the important matter of the rights of the parent, which are the divine and therefore the most efficient safeguard of the rights of the child.

Agricultural Mass Production

Fruit Growing in the Wisbech District: Some New Ideas

W E ARE ASKED to publish the following letter, which is described by the writer as "an open letter to a school-fellow":

My dear X,—Twenty years of separation seemed but a day when you and I met each other last Monday morning at Wisbech St Mary's[82] station. The two days I stayed with you in your old Georgian house in the midst of orchards are an unforgettable event in a life now darkening into night. We renewed our boyhood, not merely by telling over again the litany of our boyish pranks, but still more by reviving our boyish habit of making every subject under the sun a matter of warm and even fiery discussion. The things I had the hardihood to say to you were so new to your ears and thought, that you made me promise to set them down in writing, so that you might accept or refute them at leisure. This letter is therefore the fruit of your desire and my promise. Let me therefore begin *in nomine Domini. Amen.*

My main trouble is that you are such a good fellow; you would not deliberately wrong a worm, much less a human being, if you knew it was wrong. I have underlined these last words with fear and trembling, only because the love of truth and of you bids me ask you to look at their truth. Men who would not consciously do wrong may sometimes be unconscious of the wrong they are led or made to do. Deny this as a principle and all I shall write on these pages will be written in vain. Accept it as a principle, and you will begin to examine your conscience not about the wrongness of what is clearly wrong, but about the possible wrongness of what is seemingly right.

Now I find that you are in some ways an efficient and almost a model fruit grower. You have spent time and money in finding out the science of making fruit-trees yield their heaviest crops. You are something of an expert on chemical manures. Business methods – or, as they are called, efficiency methods – are to be seen everywhere on your estate, from the duly initialled gates of your orchards to the telephone and cash register of your office. You are looked up to by your fellow fruit growers with admiration, even if with jealousy. Men do not love you. But they love your ways, because you have made the method of growing and selling of fruit an enterprise that pays.

A night or two ago I almost irritated you when in answer to your statement that "you had made fruit-farming pay," I asked with almost equal irritation, "Pay what?" Certainly your methods of fruit-farming have paid such a dividend that whereas you began in a small way with a hand or two, you now count your acres and your fruit-harvesters by the thousand. But do you forget that there was a heavy dividend for the men who destroyed the wealth of the American forests with the rip-saw? And I was told of a man in Sussex who made it pay to ruin the weald with his pigs. It paid him; but it did not pay Sussex. It paid the timber merchants to ruin the American forests; but it did not pay America.

The question for your brain and conscience is therefore this: "I know it has paid me a dividend to add field to field, and to turn hundreds of acres of arable land in Cambridge and Norfolk into orchard. But does it pay Cambridge or Norfolk? And even if it pays Cambridge or Norfolk and me, does it pay England?" If it paid England and you to turn every acre of England into asparagus beds – would it really pay England? The wages of sin is – death. Sin pays. But it pays death. Adding "house to house, and field to field" pays. But ask the prophet who fashioned this deadly phrase what is the wages of this sorry business of adding house to house and field to field? Then curse him; not me.

Let me not so much condemn you, as condole with you. You were too soon and too deeply engaged in *making a fair return for capital*, that is, in making money, to realize that the money-measure of what pays is as transitory and therefore unscientific as the dust into which money inevitably comes. Money is not primary wealth or even secondary wealth, because it is not real wealth, but only token wealth. A country or a county, a kingdom or a farm organized on a basis of token wealth is doomed to final failure. For the moment the organization for token wealth rather than for real wealth may result in an increase of token wealth. But there is an inevitable day whenever this show of wealth passes away; and only such real wealth as has been produced remains.

Your large mass production makes your fruit farm as much a factory as the cotton-mills of Lancashire. In days when English men and women – not to say English children – can hardly afford good unadulterated

English wheaten bread, you have miles of strawberries – and flowers! As a lover of your England, ask yourself: "Is the farm of fruit and flowers the best I can do to serve the land I love?" And if by your organization on a money-basis England is the poorer, are you the richer? Who would be rich if England be poor?

But I must close my letter lest something like tears blots the words I write. Sorrow rather than anger may master me. Lest the throe of a great grief should mislead my pen into stinging you, let me canalize my sorrows into the rhythm of an economic creed.

1. I believe that human life, being a divine gift, is not adequately paid by any human dividend, but only by a divine wage.

2. I believe that "the desire of money is the root of all evil" in our economic world.

3. I believe that a life organized for money-making is the error of taking "gain to be godliness."

4. I believe that money values are false values; as money weights are false weights.

5. I believe that mass production on the land is not for the sake of the land, but for the sake of money.

6. I believe that what is called money-making is not wealth-making, but is money-getting.

7. I believe that the growing of one commodity, such as fruit or flowers, finally impoverishes the country by making it the servant of the town; whereas the town should be the servant of the country.

8. I believe that the salvation of our over-industrialized England must come from the land; but it cannot come from industrializing the land.

9. I believe that the business methods which have brought our towns to bankruptcy would bring our country to bankruptcy.

10. Finally, I believe that by organizing our land work for a market, and not for home and homestead consumption, inevitably puts the land-worker at the mercy of the market and the transport service which carries to the market.

11. I believe in God, the pattern on the Mount, who has challenged us by a life and death given to the service of mankind.

12. I believe that to serve God by serving man is not to be a slave, but a king. *Servire Deo regnare est.* God's service is kingship!

These points I offer to your friendly discussion. I shall read your answer with delight.

"O. P."

A Window in Wisbech

An Open Letter to an Old School-Fellow

MY LAST LETTER to you on Agricultural Mass Production was happy in drawing from you a long carefully reasoned statement of your case. I cannot think that the system which even your goodness is unable to redeem will find a more accredited Counsel for the Defence. You will understand that I am neither fearing nor ignoring your arguments, when I pen an instant answer to your practical question, "What, then, would you suggest?"

I therefore suggest that some day next week when your Rolls-Royce motor runs you into Wisbech (St Peter's) you will take your stand as today I have taken my stand before a window in Wisbech. The traveller for wisdom, whom the genius of Macaulay[83] had summoned from New Zealand, took his stand upon a ruined arch of London Bridge to sketch the ruins of St Paul's. At my suggestion take your stand before a window in Wisbech to detect the ruins of the land you love.

It was through the window of what my childhood called "a grocer's shop" that today I saw as in a horoscope the foundering ship of England's good estate. I was a brother of the Seer of the Isle of Patmos as I gazed at the window-pane. His authentic vision of the doom to come smote him as he saw seven golden candlesticks. I saw the doom not only of the Isle of Ely, but of the Isle of England amidst the tins and jars and card-board boxes crowding a window in Wisbech.

The first element in this apocalypse which smote me almost to the point of death in the Isle of Ely was the change of name. No longer could I name the "shops" even of a little country town as I named them in childhood. There were but few "shops." All were Stores. Noble crafts and trades were fast disappearing before the anonymous Stoics. The market towns of my childhood were lovely to look at with their streets full of noble dwelling-places, where men lived over their work; and their shop was their home, as their home was their shop. How goodly a sight was a winding street filled with signs such as "George Smith, Grocer; Elijah Jones, Shoemaker; Reuben Dassett, Harness-maker; Edward Bloxam, Innkeeper; John Bovill, Flesher; Joseph Jameson, Joiner." These music-laden litanies of Englishmen and women, of English crafts and trades are rapidly dying under the strokes of the anonymous Stores with their efficient G.H.Q. and their elaborate system of check and counter-check.

Pardon me, my dearest X—, but try to understand me when I own that whenever I see a business organized by the aid of typewriter and cash-register, I feel a chill about my heart. For many a man of today these things mean the last word in national efficiency – whatever that may mean. For me, the most efficient typewriting multiplier or cash-register is but the outward and visible sign of a diabolic system, which can succeed by supposing that everybody and especially every "hand" or "employee" is a rogue who is bent on theft. All these elaborate machines are, in their ultimate analysis, but a means for preventing "the other fellow from doing you!" England was once wittily called "a nation of shopkeepers." The pity is that England has largely become "a nation of store-keepers," where only a few own anything, and the mass of men and women are given a weekly wage for administering a typewriter and cash-register system, which looks on them as potential thieves until they are found out!

To return to the window in Wisbech. Just as John had his authentic revelation when he saw, as it were, a son of man walking amidst the seven golden candlesticks; so was I visited by withering vision as I saw, as it were, a son of England walking amidst the pots, jars, tins, and boxes in the window of a Stores in Wisbech St Peter's. Imagine my amaze at finding the land-workers of the Isle of Ely invited to season their frugal breakfast or luncheon with a slice or two of bacon from Denmark! When I came to think of it I remembered how few pigs of any breed I had seen in the Isle of Ely. For a moment or two I began to ask the reason of this dearth of English pigs and this plentifulness of Danish bacon amidst the people of business habits. But my brain reeled; until in sheer self-defence I began, as it were, to recount the seven golden candlesticks, that is, the pots, jars, tins, and cardboard boxes in a window in Wisbech.

Around me lay one of the most fertile lands not in England merely, but in the world – a soil so helped by our winds and rains and sunshine as to yield a greater number of products, and in greater quantity than almost any land under the sun. Yet that very day when I had tea with the gentlemen from the University of Cambridge, who were giving up their holidays to help the gentlemen and ladies who had come fruit-picking, the

substance we poured out on our bread was not Wisbech butter (a most
delicate product!) but margarine, which we owed to the generosity of
some vegetable plot belonging to a soap boiler in Western Africa!

William Cobbett, in his immortal *Rural Rides*, had taught me how
to look on rural England with the sharp critical eyes of love. I therefore
took an apocalyptic valuation of preserved meat products which were
stacked up in the window of Wisbech. Within sight of some of the richest
grazing land of the world I saw the "finest peasantry of Europe" hyp-
notized into buying tins of meat that may have been in store at Chicago
or the Argentine for some months or years; thereupon I began to think
furiously about our "modern means of transport." When a boy at school I
had been taught to look upon Arkwright[84] and Stephenson[85] as practically
of more importance to England than, say, John the Baptist or Simon, son
of John – not to mention a more sacred Name. But of late years I had
awakened to the simple principles that what lets-out usually lets-in. If
railways and tar-macadam roads give us a foreign market, they equally
make us a foreign market. Now ask any level-headed fruit farmer, especially if he is on the County Council of Ely, what is the chief burden on
farm produce, and he will reply, "After the labourers wages, which are not
quite a family wage, the chief charge is railway rates and highway rates.
We are paying high for luxurious high roads, which are no great advantage to anything but to luxurious motor cars." Then I gave up thinking
about modern transport services, and turned my eyes to other phenomena
in the window at Wisbech. Heaven had helped my eyes by sending me
to an hotel which, having its own garden, could give its clients one of the
world's most delicious foods and sweetmeats – English home-made jam.
Had I not eaten – indeed, over-eaten English plum jam and gooseberry
jam worth a king's ransom? Yet the window in Wisbech was full of
glucose masquerading as jam in one of the world's most fertile orchards.
Nay, did I not see tinned pears from California, and tinned peaches from
Australia – my friend at my side grunted testily "and tinned ices from
the devil!" Thereupon I swooned before a window in Wisbech. When I
awoke you were at my side. I looked out of another window in Wisbech,
which seemed but the foot of the bed on which I lay. An old mullioned
gable window across the yard bore the date 1601. Athwart the gable grew
a vine. I saw the England that once was; and my heart leaped as I thought
of the England that is to be.

Yours faithfully,

"O. P."

Wisdom at Cardiff

THE BRITISH ASSOCIATION has been holding its yearly meeting at Cardiff.

The town itself gave the men of science an opportunity of wisdom. Last year when the British Association met at Bournemouth, their President, the Hon. Sir Charles Parsons,[86] sought to thrill them by the old Utilitarian view of the "Utility and Progress" of science. He was almost dithyrambic in describing the marvellous achievements of science during the war. Perhaps he might have sung a quieter note if he had remembered Ruskin's[87] definition of wealth "as that which serves human life," and not like war science, human death. In the end this President of the British Association proposed that at a cost of £5,000,000 they should sink a shaft to the depth of twelve miles – in search of power! Perhaps he could not be expected to remember that since 1870, the year of *national education*, some 3,000,000 people have left the land, some 4,600,000 acres have ceased to be tilled, and the yearly education bill is now £78,000,000. When the British Association met at Bournemouth in September, 1919, the dawn of victory was still too red in the sky for any President of the Association to forbear cock crowing.

But Cardiff was an opportunity for wisdom. No one could steam into it by train, between its blackened factories – the thumb marks of wealth – without feeling like a thief breaking into a house, not through the garden door, but through the coal-cellar. When the collective scientific wisdom of Britain stepped out of the train into the streets of Cardiff they were welcomed by a dead wall, mean houses, and streets littered with the offal of a week's (or was it a month's?) city life. As they had just passed through the rich farm lands and orchards of Hereford or Monmouth, Cardiff, merely as a modern city, gave them an opportunity of seeing the physical failures of modern utilitarian science.

Moreover, the state of things in Cardiff gave them a much more valuable opportunity of seeing the economic and psychological failures of modern utilitarian science. Cardiff was not only mean and dirty in its wealth (!); but Cardiff was on strike; in spite of the collective science of the British Association. Cardiff is no doubt proud of its electric tram service, which, with its endless supply of Welsh steam-coal, it can run, no doubt, more cheaply than can any other British city of the same population. Yet Cardiff's electric tram service had broken down. It was not that the Welsh steam-coal had suddenly failed to burn, or that the electric current could not fly along the wires, or that the tram wheels refused to go round. It was that the tram-men would not work. Moreover, these tram-men refused to work, not because they were too tired or too hungry for their job, nor because they were too ill-paid, but because they took pity on a handful of road-menders who thought they had a right to more pay. In other words, Cardiff offered to the British Association an opportunity of learning economic and therefore political wisdom from the dislocation caused by a group of men discontented with their wages, that is, with their token-wealth.

Out on the land farmers were beginning to fear lest their pay-master, the Land, would not give them the living wage of a good harvest. But against the earth and sky even in their surliest, wettest moods, a farmers strike is unavailing. Strikes are a city parasite; sometimes sporadically found on the land.

That wisdom came to some of the men and women of science who saw Cardiff in its strike may be gathered from the address of the President of the Economic Section, Dr. J. H. Clapham, of King's College, Cambridge. Perhaps he could not fail to contrast the old mediaeval agriculturalism which had produced Cambridge and King's College, Cambridge, with the new industrialism which had produced Cardiff and the railway station, Cardiff. A man going down from Cambridge to Cardiff, like the man going down from Jerusalem to Jericho, would naturally fall, or seem to fall, among thieves, who, would despoil him of his goods and leave him half-dead.

Being a historian, this President of the Economic Section was fully equipped to be a prophet. He contrasted the year 1920 with the year 1820, and the Great Prussian War with the great Napoleonic Wars. He backed his timid prophecies with the figures of the state of things when these wars had come to an end.

"Demobilization in France presented few of the problems familiar to us. *Probably not one man in ten demobilized was a pure wage-earner. The rest had had links with the soil.* The land neglected during the war was crying out for labour, and every man had his place, even if it was a servile place in rural society.

"Things were different in England; but our demobilization problems were smaller than those of our Continental allies or enemies. Early in 1817 Lord Castlereagh stated that 300,000 soldiers and sailors had been discharged. For these men no provision whatever was made. They were simply thrown on the labour market; and the vast majority of them were ex-wage-earners, or potential wage-earners, industrial, mercantile and agricultural. It is not surprising that the years from 1815 to 1820 were both economically and politically the most wretched, difficult and dangerous in modern English history.

"If the experience of Europe after Waterloo was on the whole of good augury for agricultural states, and especially for agricultural states with a competent Central Government, for the industrialized modern world that experience was less encouraging. Great Britain alone was partially industrialized in 1815–1820; and Great Britain, though victorious, suffered acutely. It was as yet too early to work out a parallel between this post-war commercial and industrial slump and the slump that followed the war of 1914–1918, for we had not yet had it. But it was coming. More certainly in the United States than in England; but pretty certainly here also. It would begin in the field of finance, spreading to industry, and would give us a bad spell of unemployment comparable with the unemployment of the post-war period a century ago; but more dangerous owing to the high standard of living to which people have become accustomed."

This President of the Economic Section of the British Association was preaching, perhaps unconsciously, to his fellow-scientists a sermon on the dangers of their science. Only a year before his sermon, another sermon by the Hon. Sir Charles Parsons had cheered these same scientists on to the crusade of using their science to bring in the reign of industrialism. Dr. J. H. Clapham's crusade was the reverse of this; it looked with accurate eye on the hurt done by war to the victors almost more than to the vanquished; and learning wisdom from past mistakes it sought to retrieve these mistakes by the simple war cry, "Back to the Land."

And Cardiff, with its steam coal, its token wealth, its profiteers, it, tawdriness, its slums, its dimming Celtic vision, was there at the Professor's hand to enforce his prophecy.

The Widowed Land

Since 1871 the number of people engaged in the cultivation of the soil has gone down by 700,000–600,000 men, I believe. That means probably that you have a population of 3,000,000 less than you had on that date, directly associated with agriculture.

—Mr. Lloyd George, October 22, 1919.

MORE AND MORE do we feel that the dominant study of all Catholic Social Study Circles should be the land. We are even opening to the view that the land should be the main study of all the apostolic men who are hungering for the spread of Christ's kingdom on earth.

Thinkers formed by the principles of the *Rerum Novarum* are beginning to realize that the social ill, inasmuch as it has an economic cause, is springing from the growth of the industrial town and the widowhood of the land. Now as genius is the gift of putting the first (or best) things in the first place, any attempt to make the best of secondary things will sooner or later lead to social bankruptcy.

Yet at the present time almost all our national efforts are towards doing still better by that machine production which is giving us not of primaries, such as wheat, oats, cows, sheep – and children, but secondaries such as oil-driven liners, self-binders, tinned foods and model flats. Our schemes of reconstruction have no other vision than to perpetuate social sores by a liberal dressing with social anti-septics. Of this we are even proud. Thus Birmingham is proud that by intense work in welfare centres it has brought down its high infant death rate in the poorer neighbourhoods by a slight percentage, when it ought to be humbled to reflect that if there were not these poorer neighbourhoods there would not be a high infant death-rate to bring down.

The Social Worker's Main Task

The chief duty of modern social workers is not to disinfect the industrial towns but to disperse them; not to establish expensive health centres for dealing with the millions of slum dwellers; but to restore these millions to the widowed land.

We therefore urged that the problem of how to give back to the land her lost millions should be the chief problem of all Catholic Social Study Guilds. Not otherwise than by making fit restitution to the land can the social evils be stemmed.

The Housing Question

To be explicit let us take some few of the main social problems:

1. HOUSING.—It seems quite clear that the industrial towns, with their industrial methods of production, are bankrupt in the matter of Housing. As the country lacks at least 1,000,000 houses, the cost of erection at present rates would be £1,000,000,000 (a thousand million pounds)! Talk as people may, the country has no intention of making the outlay. Birmingham has some 50,000 houses condemned as unfit for people to live in. But the people will have to live in them. Land is dear, labour is dear, materials are dear. But granted a return to the land – all these elements of cost would shrink down to a practical level. If the land cannot solve this problem, nothing else can.

Cold Storage

2. FOOD.—The advent of cold storage has nearly ruined our food supplies! According to Mr. H. Adams, Vice-President of the United London Meat Trading Association, the market has never been in such a condition in his experience of over fifty years. He says: "We have had to beg for inferior meat, and when we have got it, bad as it is, we have had to take something worse with it – ten very inferior frozen sheep."

The poorer consumers have had to buy tinned food at exorbitant prices – or putrid mutton. Yet the other day at a meeting of these Captains of the Cold Storage they drank the toast "The Empire and Cold Storage." Whilst, then, the facts are that these methods of industrialism have given food of worse quality and in lesser quantity, it seems futile to discuss the matter except on a basis of "Back to the Land."

Industrialism and Health

3. HEALTH.—If the industrial town which has impoverished the land is now necessarily impoverishing the town-dwellers in their homes and food, we need not be surprised that it is finally impoverishing their health. The medical returns compiled during the war-recruiting showed the land to be the source of the fittest population. Yet we think we have done a stroke of genius by organizing a most costly Ministry of Health whose chief function will be to perpetuate the main source of ill-health, the industrial town.

Ministry of Health and Density of Population

Already this Ministry has shown its anxiety to take the financial or industrial outlook. It has lowered the L.C.C. scale of height for rooms. It has sanctioned grants for flats – with roof playgrounds for children! In other words it has sanctioned the penning of town-dwellers into areas of denser and denser population. Then in order to lessen the high death rate which it has created, it will establish expensive welfare centres with a host of officials. This is called National Efficiency. But there are a few sensible folk who look upon it as mental deficiency of a singularly malignant character. They also look upon it as almost equally a sign of mental defect to study this problem of health except as a problem of "Back to the Land."

4. EDUCATION.—Already the educational system is breaking down. Its introduction in 1870 corresponds with that leakage from the land to the town which is now our greatest national danger. The educational methods are now about as futile as they could well be. Children grow up with a knowledge not of things but of tokens. They are being taught to

be at home with machines; and therefore to be slaves of machines. Some town-children on going into the country have wondered how people could live in the country, because there were no shops. Yet town children are given what is tragically called "Nature Studies"! How palpably is it a waste of time to discuss education apart from the land!

The law therefore should favour ownership; and its policy should be to induce as many as possible to become owners. Many excellent results will follow.

1. First of all, property will certainly become more equitably divided...

2. ...the greater abundance of the fruits of the earth.

3. ...Men would cling to the country in which they were born."—(Pope Leo XIII, *Rerum Novarum*).

Souls and the Land

D URING EASTER I had the adventure of my life. Laying aside my
black, twentieth century clerical clothes, and wearing only the
old black and white habit that came to England seven hundred
years ago, I and a beloved priest-friend went a-preaching through one
of the English counties. We hardly knew what would befall us day by
day. Indeed, we were expecting the unexpected, since we looked upon
ourselves as "God's spies" sent forward from the main army to see the lie
and wealth and life of the land.

No little part of an unforgettable week was the daily fare of talk
between us. A week's release from letters and newspapers gave us time
and chance to see God's revelation written, as agnostics would have it
written, in the sky. Once, by walking ten miles before Mass and breakfast, we had a schooling in prophecy better than the whole of the morning
Press. Visits to Catholic families working on their little holdings added to
our overcrowded food for thought. So that when we were alone together
trudging from one of God's outposts to another our wallets of talk-stuff
were full to overflowing. Indeed, so many ideas sought an outlet in our
speech that again and again our dialogue became a subtle duet in which
two priests strove to talk and to listen at the same time.

Memories of the Past

The gentle hills and wide valleys where the God of the hills and
valleys had summoned us were so scented with the memories of penal
times that even during the bright Easter sunshine we seemed to march
in step with a white-robed company of martyrs. One day I walked alone
some five-and-twenty miles across the country. Yet not alone! Never for
a moment was I bereaved of the mirthful battalion of martyrs and confessors who became wayfarers at my side. Every farmhouse by the way
seemed to be the home of a Catholic yeoman who sheltered a Massing

priest. Every country seat had for us its priest's hiding-place to baffle the pursuivants. We were visiting the battle-fields of England where one of the most stubborn and unequal wars was waged by a handful of land-dwellers against the most powerful Government in the world.

But to the two priests who pilgrimed amidst this battle-ground it seemed that another war was calling for the Catholic yeoman and plough-man to save us from defeat. Towns giving the poorer Catholics, "that is, the majority" (Lacordaire) no alternative between the heroic virtue of abstention or the mortal sin of Neo-Malthusian birth-control were no longer part of the Catholic defence against paganism, but part of the pagan attack against Catholicism

The Country and the Church

Alone the country with its homes and homesteads, its settled prop-erty, its round of world-enriching work, its touch with the realities of sea and land and sky, could save the Church from the literal fulfilment of our Blessed Lord's almost disheartening prophecies of the world's ending. The joy of seeing Catholic homes where at any time of day the priest-shepherd could see and speak to his flock was chilled by the thought that the truths we saw as clearly as we saw the tilled land, the fowl pens, the styes, the byres, the barns, were not truths to the town-folk, but the dreams of men unmoored from reality.

A Lesson From America

Yet the dismay that smote us on our return to the realities of Ealing, Westbourne Grove, Paddington, and Camden Town[88] was suddenly lifted by a brother voice that hailed us from across the Atlantic Ocean. The Gospel which W. Cobbett, G. K. Chesterton,[89] H. Belloc,[90] and others have preached to thin audiences and dwindling wheat-fields, Dr. O'Hara[91] (in America) has discovered and has just begun to preach in the United States. After the true American manner, he reinforces his gospel with statistics; not the uncertain statistics of the individual observer, but the official statistics of the national census of 1906–1916. These figures are unsettling enough to occasion a new Church Council of Baltimore or Westminster. They prove that during the ten years 1906–1916:

The population of the United States increased 17 per cent.
The Protestant Churches increased 19 per cent.
The Catholic Church increased 10 per cent.

These figures are so startling that Dr. O'Hara has sought to interpret them. His interpretation seems to confirm the view we ourselves took after an examination of the facts in the United States.

The Crowding of Catholics in Towns

He points out that whereas three-fourths of the Catholics live in towns and one-fourth live in the country, the Protestant church-goers have but one fourth of their number in the towns and three-fourths in the country! His counsel is definite, and therefore challenging: "There is only one way out: through the systematic fostering of Catholic rural life."

What Dr. O'Hara has proved as a thesis by the census return of the most highly industrialized country in the world an anonymous writer has set to literary prose in what I would call "an open letter to a Catholic Master-Shepherd." Those who know the hand-printing of St Dominic's Press,[92] Ditchling, Sussex, will find the case for the land put with force and literature in a pamphlet entitled *Missions; or, Sheepfolds and Shambles, by a Sheep.* More prophetic insight finds its place in this slender book than we have seen since Cobbett. A few years ago the wisdom of this "sheep" would have been taken as the bleatings of folly But the thing called "worldly wisdom" and "industrial supremacy," after waging a war which has left us bankrupt, has gone on to wage a peace which is making us beggared. The artificial wealth which we had and held too long for our national soberness of thought is now taking wing and leaving us undeluded. It is a moment apt for reality and truth.

A Vital Truth

And a week's spy-work in the almost untilled land of England has confirmed unto us the truth that to convert England means to convert not its overcrowded towns but its undertilled and under-peopled countrysides, where homes and homesteads alone can safeguard the freedom with which Christ has made us free.

The Social Need of Flying the Occasions of Sin

An Open Letter To A Young Priest

YOUR REQUEST that I should offer you some guidance in social matters lays on me the hard duty of telling you the truth, without deep concern for the use to which the truth may be put by your convictions or emotions. On the whole I am glad that some little part of your well-earned holiday you are going to spend at one or other of the summer meetings on social matters. Your giving up of time that could be spent in the sun and on the land or sea is a heroic self-sacrifice which cannot fail of its fruit.

It would be difficult to point out the precise advantage you will have gained over those of your set who will take the good things of land and sea with unstinted hand.

Probable Disappointment

You are likely to come away from some, if not most, of these meetings on social matters with a sense of depression bordering on despair. You will recall with excess of bitterness the Master's reproof of those who "think that in their much speaking they will be heard." You will be tempted to condemn all these social activities as unconscious enemies of much doing by their overmuch speaking.

Two thoughts will tend to thwart your despair. You will remember that speaking may be the forth-telling of truth. Now, if truth itself is an achievement it will be easily seen how true is the mystic phrase, "In the beginning was the Word." You and I are looking for social salvation only through an Exodus. We should not forget how often Moses needed to speak before his enslaved kinsmen could see that the desert was better than the flesh-pots of Egypt.

Despair and Action

Again, the sense of despair is, or to a man of action can be, the beginning of action. A man must be without hope, and indeed without sense, if he gives up his quest merely because he has come upon the sign "No Road." Much of our social speaking is but a vernacular warning that this or that scheme ends with the pit.

The Call of Duty

Take your stand, then, upon the authentic diagnosis of Pope Leo XIII: "A remedy must be found, and found quickly, for the misery and wretchedness pressing so heavily and so unjustly on the vast majority of the working-classes." These words of a Pope, so worthy to set beside the "woes" of our Blessed Lord, are but a plain call to the duty of "flying the occasions of sin." Let me explain.

1. By the working-classes is meant not merely the hand-workers, but even many of the head-workers – if, indeed, these two classes can be distinguished. It is part of the modern social evil that our educational methods – never the product of the Catholic Church – have given us millions of men and women fitted for nothing but office work with figures and typing gear. These clerical classes are as undeniably within the purview of the Pope's words as are the men and women generally recognized as working classes.

At the Mercy of Employers

Indeed, if we recognize how these vast clerical classes in their unorganized condition are wholly at the mercy of their employers we cannot deny them the right to be considered a group within those working-classes whom Pope Leo XIII's words describe.

2. Insist, in season and out of season, that for the vast majority of these working-classes, manual and clerical, our present system is a proximate occasion of mortal sin. Your experience of town-life may be as yet too

scanty to verify this fact. But soon you will be unable to deny that, with wages as they are and house-rents as they are, and evil propaganda as it is, life for the normal man and woman is a proximate occasion of sin.

Our Present System and the Workers

I will put it in the concrete. A young clerk in the city has just married. After a good deal of search he has found a small flat of three rooms in a healthy neighbourhood. For this flat he pays £75 a year – say £1 10s. a week. His landlord stands to him almost in the character of a benefactor. Now this kind benefactor, in one of his friendly talks with the young clerk, gives a polite but unmistakable hint that "if there is an addition to the family" their agreement will be at an end. That same afternoon the post brings him a copy of an artistically printed magazine explaining – mortal sin. Again, X. is the father of five children. He finds himself almost forty and out of work through the failure of his firm. His slender savings are rapidly lessening, as every week he must spend some thirty shillings upon rent before he has bought food for his children's mouth or clothes for their back. His friends, who are mostly non-Catholic, tell him he is reckless in having a family. He begins to ask himself if in conscience he can bring into existence another being whom he can provide for only by neglecting those whom he has already brought into existence. In other words, can he beget children – unto starvation ?

Dominating Economic Facts

3. As these two typical (and hypothetical) cases are economic facts, they dominate the social question. Full family life must be the acid test of any system calling itself civilization. But under our present system the possibility of full family life is practically and explicitly dead. Facts and assertions, deeds and words, are agreed that our system of town civilization gives the ordinary working man, clerical or manual, but two alternatives. As wages and rent are, there is no possibility for the average working man to have the average family. In order to avoid this average family only two courses are now open to him. He may exercise birth-control by

abstinence, which is sinless, or by the Neo-Malthusian methods of mortal sin. His only choice is therefore between mortal sin and what is for the average individual heroic virtue. In other words, the town civilization of today is for the vast majority of the married classes a proximate occasion of sin. But it is the teaching of the Church that we must fly the proximate occasions of sin. To remain in unnecessary occasions of sin is to be guilty of the sin we should fly.

A Quick Change in the System Necessary

4. Ask again and again and again, What are we Catholics doing to change the system which Pope Leo XIII told us we must change quickly? Are we doing much when in this country alone there are some two million unemployed, clerical and manual, and many more millions under-employed, with the result that Neo-Malthusian propaganda is spreading rapidly, even amongst our own people? We priests should and would be the first to recognize that if our house is built over an open sewer we do not meet the circumstance by laying in a stock of medicines – or even by organizing a Ministry of Health. Many of the expedients suggested at our summer meetings are but attempts to cure the defects of bad circumstances, not by a change of circumstances, but by a change of medicine. If only you can draw your audience's attention to the necessity for nations, like individuals, to fly the occasions of sin, you will soon pass from discussing that Race Suicide which is the shortest way out; and you will begin to discuss economic evil in terms of the city, where these evils are forced to breed, and the country, into which they can be brought only by infection from the town. In other words, you will discuss the exodus which alone can justify us before the God who gave the land into our keeping.

Is It Socialism?

THOSE OF US who have long since jettisoned the painted thrills of fiction for the wild realities of Blue Books, Parliamentary Minutes, Medical Officers Reports, and Unemployment statistics are at a loss to account for the chill welcome given to a report issued on January 9th, 1924. Perhaps the modern political Press deliberately seeks by flagrant sporting items to keep the masses from thinking about the deadlier sport, and indeed war, which is raging in the land. Be that as it may, we would call our readers from their sport or their prayers to consider the final "Report of the Departmental Committee of the Board of Agriculture on the distribution and prices of Agricultural Produce."

Such strong denunciations and such revolutionary suggestions find their way into the Report that some men who might be called higher critics would find in it, as they find in the *Rerum Novarum*, a nidus of Socialism! But, as in the one case they are reassured by being reminded that it is the official utterance of a Pope, Leo XIII, so in the other case they may be reassured by remembering that the Report is issued under a Conservative Government and by a committee presided over by the Marquis of Linlithgow![93] If this is not sufficiently reassuring, we ask: "Where is balsam to be found?"

There is music – "the dull music of the distant drum" – in the noble things about whose fate the Departmental Committee sought tidings. The group of experts under the leadership of the Marquis of Linlithgow went in search of all that befalls "milk and milk products, fruit and vegetables, meat, poultry, and eggs, and cereals, flour, and bread." It was a noble quest; an adventure as thrilling as an Arctic Expedition; a sport more exciting and vital than any cup-tie.

The general conclusion of this Conservative Government Departmental Report is a piece of sober English almost exciting to revolution. "The Committee reiterate their view" (given in an interim report) that the difference between the prices obtained "by the producer and those charged to the consumer is far too wide, and that the profits of certain classes of distributors are unduly large and should be reduced." These plain words contain (1) an empiric fact, and (2) a revolutionary recommendation. Gentle reader, read the words again and again until you realize the fact and agree with the recommendation.

Here are several aspects and statements of the fact.

The spread between producers and consumers prices is unjustifiably wide.

Food producers are inadequately remunerated, while the agencies standing between them and the consumer remain apparently undisturbed in the enjoyment of their reward.

Whilst the profits earned by agricultural producers have been seriously curtailed by the price changes of the last two years, the profits of distributors and the wages of the workers in the transport and distributive trades show in many cases an increase of 100 per cent., or even more, above the pre-war level.

"The agencies engaged in the transport of produce from the farm to the home have been able to pass on their costs to the consumer.

"CONSEQUENTLY BY MAINTAINING HIGH PRICES THEY HAVE TO SOME EXTENT LIMITED THE QUANTITY OF GOODS WHICH THE CONSUMERS COULD OBTAIN!!

This cannot be regarded as a service to the nation.

..."It is better that a readjustment should be made by the trade itself rather than by legislative enactment, with all its deterrent effects upon initiative and development

"In regard to transport, it is again emphasized that a revision of railway rates is overdue.

"Individual traders and groups of traders are in some cases still making higher profits than are warranted by the services they perform. These profits should be reduced...." "In some trades there are now too many agencies engaged in the process of distribution."

It is a consolation to realize that these revolutionary facts and recommendations have been issued by a Conservative, and indeed by a Business Government. Their appearance on the eve of a possible Labour Government is timely to a point of niceness. The meagre litany we have compiled from the Report would provide ample thought-food for a

Catholic Social Week. To the present writer the group of statements he has strung together contains in solution all those economic conditions which are now giving us the heavy immoral, anti-social harvest of Neo-Malthusianism. Again and again we have urged our Catholic thinkers to realize that with the necessities of food and housing at their present level the Neo-Malthusian seems the only practical and sympathetic social apostle.

1. The Report is largely an indictment (a) of the Transport, and (b) of the Distributing agencies. In other words, the Report is an indictment of what the modern world makes its chief boast! The mechanical transport by land and sea and air, the modern market and multiple stores. Economists are gradually learning that "conveniences can be a great inconvenience." A civilization which has concentrated on distribution and not on production and consumption must infallibly end in bankruptcy.

2. St Thomas and the Schoolmen would comment on the verified fact that the trader as such is not of primary social need, that he is merely an accidental need, and that, unlike the maker of real wealth, he practises a craft that is less honourable. The Report is a dismal plea that this trader has almost strangled the producer.

3. The words we have honoured with capitals are a terrible indictment of a civilization largely concerned with transport and trading. They give the sanction of authority to the economic law that monopolies tend to make profits not by increasing output but by decreasing output! In other words, monopolies tend to CA'CANNY[94] methods. In a previous article we called attention to the thousands of tons of potatoes destroyed last year in England because there had been a plentiful harvest.

4. The Report asks the voluntary traders and transport agencies voluntarily to lessen their profits – or there will be "legislative enactments." Is it Socialism?

The Joy of Poverty

Thoughts in the Stable of Bethlehem

THE DUMB OX OF AQUINO has said of the Babe Jesus so many things true and noble that we wonder if he was not own-brother to the ox that watched and warmed the Babe in the manger.

Praises of Bethlehem Poverty

Let us listen to him singing in his own literary plain-song the praises of this Bethlehem poverty. "It was fitting for Christ to live a life of poverty in this world. First, because this was in keeping with the duty of preaching.... Wherefore the Lord Himself when sending the Apostles to preach said to them (Matt. x 9), 'Do not possess gold nor silver.'

"Secondly, because, just as He took upon Himself the death of the body in order to bestow spiritual life on us, so did He bear bodily poverty in order to enrich us spiritually, according to II Cor. viii 9: 'You know the grace of our Lord Jesus Christ.... He became poor for your sakes that through His poverty you might be rich.'

"Thirdly, lest if He were rich His preaching might be ascribed to cupidity. Wherefore Jerome says that if the disciples had been possessed of wealth they had seemed to preach for gain, not for the salvation of mankind. And the same reason applies to Christ.

"Fourthly, that the more lowly He seemed by reason of His Poverty, the greater might the power of His Godhead be shown to be. Hence in a sermon of the Council of Ephesus we read...'For this reason did He choose a poor maid for His mother, a poorer birthplace; for this reason did He live in want. Learn this from the manger.'"†

---

† *Summa Theologica*, III, Q. 40, Art.3.

The Poverty of Christ

No wonder that the birth of the Child in this consummate poverty of Bethlehem is paradoxically set amidst the five joyful Mysteries. The poverty of Jesus Christ was not an end in itself, but a means towards an end. It was not a mere "doing without" or "going without." It became a necessity to the Word made Flesh as soon as He set His mind on telling the world the good news of God's love and God's forgiveness. Worldly riches – or, as St Thomas would say, bodily riches – make an indifferent preacher of spiritual riches. Gold and silver are sometimes of use to the Apostle; but never of primary use. Wealth is always a dangerous servant of the Apostle; and a still more dangerous master.

The Example in the Crib and on the Cross

The voluntary – or, as our forefathers called it, the wilful – poverty of Bethlehem is the voluntary doing with as little as possible in order to bestow on others as much as possible. In His Crib, and still more on His Cross, Jesus gave us the example not so much of a poor man contented with his poverty, as of a rich man discontented with his riches. It was part of the plan of the Incarnation to show us the ideal of poverty, which we might state in economic terms thus: "Consume as little as you need and produce as much as you can." Men who consume, and control in order to consume, as much as they can whilst producing as little as they need are the impoverishment of the world. Their life leaves the world poorer than they found it. Only their death is a deliverance. But those who use for their life and work only what little they need, in order to produce things of body and spirit, are the enrichment of the world. They leave the world richer than they found it. And as their life was the world's gain, their death is a loss.

The Poverty of the Stable

At Bethlehem the Son of God took from man less, perhaps, than any babe had or has ever taken. He who shared His cradle with the Ass and the Ox can hardly be said to have taken a sufficiency for childbirth. He came into the world almost less as a man-child than as an ass's colt or as a winter lamb. The wilful poverty of the stable, with its gloom, squalor, and stench, is a heroic going without the common necessaries of birth. Yet this dearth of birth's necessaries, this Bethlehem-poverty, is God's simple apparatus for the enrichment of the world. Everything about the stable is rationed with almost divine parsimony – except God's gifts to men. The Child, the Mother of the Child, the Foster-father of the Child in their poverty make a perfect part with the poverty of the Cave. Yet God, the Artist, contrives with these scantiest and simplest of materials to fashion a masterpiece for all time. God, the Prodigal Father of a Prodigal Son, contrives to squander all the Father's and the Son's substance in a far-off land! And as the Son's stripes have been our healing, His spendthrift has been our enriching.

The Young Man with Great Possessions

Only once did anyone come to Jesus and after speech with Him go away sad. This was the young man who had great desires to have life everlasting. But he had also "great possessions." He did not know that for him the way to the joy of life was to accept the challenge of Jesus: "Go, sell whatsoever thou hast, and give to the poor, and thou shalt have treasure in Heaven. And come, follow Me"(Mark x 21). He did not realize that this invitation to follow the poor Babe of Bethlehem, the poor Man of Galilee, the poor Outcast of Golgotha, was a call to enter the narrow path of perfect joy. He could not leave the things which sooner or later would leave him. He clung to his great possessions on earth rather than seek treasure in Heaven, and left the joy of wilful poverty and the following of Jesus for the sadness of wilful wealth and the service of Mammon.

The Land and Unemployment

A s the next few years — or months? — may see no attempt to deal with the questions of unemployment and the land, it is imperative that Catholics, who alone have the ultimate principles of solution, shall also have the proximate principles of solution.

Unemployment – The Land

Our first discovery is the principle that these two questions are, perhaps, fundamentally one. In other words, "men are unemployed because the land is unemployed." There is even a striking parallelism between the two questions. Thus the evil of unemployment is made worse by the evil of under-employment. Not only are there some million and a half who are doing nothing, and, indeed, are paid for doing nothing, but there are some two millions doing little, and being paid for doing little. In most of the great industries the employees are not working full-time. All this is an incalculable loss to the real wealth of the country, even though men are not always conscious of this loss as they are conscious of other losses. After the short railway strike of 1919 there were experts who gave us a harrowing statement of the work hours that had been lost to the country. But who can calculate the work hours lost in the seven years since the war, during which time a million and a quarter men have been standing idle every day, and some three millions have been idle part of every day?

Men and Land Idle

As it is with the living worker, so it is with the land from which alone the worker has his living. As there are now a million and a half men standing idle, so there are millions of acres of English soil standing idle. Moreover, as there are millions of English workers underworking, so are there millions of English acres under-tilled. To the lover of England even a railway journey through this land has thoughts too deep for tears – or curses. This land is amongst the richest in the world. It is inhabited by people who are counted amongst the most intelligent in the world. Yet this national intelligence, which has organized the marvels of under-water sailing and air-flight and wireless telegraphy, has left the land as undeveloped as if the land-dwellers were mentally deficient and not mentally efficient.

For the moment, therefore, let us note the parallelism between the two problems of the Unemployed and the Land, in the surmise that these two so kindred problems may prove to be one.

Agriculture *v.* Machinery

A further principle is that "machine and factory organization is not as efficient as agricultural organization for dealing with unemployment." But we add the necessary condition, that it must be a genuinely agricultural organization, and not that worst of all economic diseases, an industrialized agricultural organization, which produces not for home consumption, but for market-selling!

We admit, at the outset, that such an industrial organization of agriculture, with its long distances between production and consumption, is as economically unstable and vulnerable as a small army operating with a long line of communication between its fighting front and its base.

But a genuinely agricultural organization, where the areas of production and consumption are practically co-terminous, has no equal as an efficient economic unit for creating real wealth and preventing unemployment. The ultimate economic cause of this may be found in the ultimate unit of the organization. In a land organization, with its simple elements of soil and toil, the ultimate objective unit is the land. In a factory industrial organization, with its machinery, the ultimate unit is the machine. But, whereas the land is plastic in its power of absorbing toil, the machine is practically static.

A Machine's Limits

A machine as such cannot employ more than a certain number of hands. Moreover, the more efficient the machine, the fewer hands it will employ. This principle is now so undeniable that some of the economists even of the Labour Party are enunciating the principle that machinery should either not be made more efficient, or its output should be artificially restricted – lest labour starve!

But in contrast with this limited power of the machine to employ labour in creating wealth is the almost unlimited power of the land. For all those who do not at once see this far-reaching principle England is there as an object-lesson. Since 1870 as many workers have left the land as now stand idle round the Labour Exchanges. Yet even in 1870 England was a highly under-tilled land. There was a good deal of mass production, but there was practically no intensive production. Moreover, there was everywhere the financial incubus of the market and the price, which was gradually driving out the homestead and home consumption. In other words, the less efficient was ousting the more efficient economic organization.

A False Conclusion

It is not easy to see through the entanglements of modern business methods the natural simplicities of an agricultural organization. Even the tillers of the soil have gradually become so warped by town methods of marketing and money-making as not to see the wood for the trees. Thus government Ministers of Agriculture and secretaries of Farmers' or Labourers' Associations will be heard to deny that the land could more easily be organized to absorb all our unemployed than could any other industry. In making this denial they are arguing quite consistently. But they are arriving at a false conclusion by arguing from the falsehood in an ambiguous principle. If we ask them the fateful question: "Can you so organize your land as to absorb our unemployed?" they will reply: "No. We cannot." But this denial is based on the ambiguity of the word organize. It is apparent that this word may mean (a) the organization of the work; or (b) the organization of the wage. In other words, to organize may mean the real organization or the financial organization. These two are different and separable. Thus the Panama Canal was for a long time financially organized before it was really organizable. On the other hand, the real organization of national house-building is quite simple; but the financial organization of our national house-building baffles even our financial geniuses and our most disinterested statesman.

Back to the Land

Now the real organization of the land of England for the absorption of our unemployed is an elementary problem in agriculture. It is not to be compared to the difficulty solved by the military authorities during the war, when they suddenly absorbed some seven or eight million men. There is not a countryside, there is scarcely a Rural District Council in England which could not successfully undertake the real organization of twice as many as its quota needed to absorb all the unemployed. Moreover, this absorption would produce real primary wealth such as food, clothing, housing; and not mere secondary wealth such as highways, thoroughfares, and means of transport. When, therefore, farmers say that they could not organize the land so as to absorb the unemployed they do not mean "We cannot find work for the unemployed to do," but "We cannot find wages for their work." It is the financial, and not the real, organization they shirk.

So simple and subtle is Nature that no man-made device can be her equal in meeting fluctuations of workers and work. No machine will depreciate so little if left standing idle. No machine can deal so successfully with a sudden influx of workers. The machine has only a limited capacity both in accommodation and function. It cannot employ more than a small group, unless the shifts are shortened. It cannot undertake any other than the specialized operation for which it was designed. But a tract of land in England can exist with a handful of workers; or can keep a worker or two for every acre. Moreover, it can produce every kind of real wealth from the stone that built Salisbury Minster to the wool that makes the world's best homespuns and the wheat and grapes that may become the Sacrifice of a World Redeemed.

The Catholics of England

met one of the fiercest and most effective persecutions in history by flying
to the land. When the persecution ceased and Catholics, like commerce,
shifted their centre from the land to the towns, Catholics did not grow in
proportion to the growth of population. Immigration from Catholic Ireland seemed to hide the dwindling of their numbers. Neither the urban
life nor the industrial atmosphere fitted in with their spiritual mentality.
At length they, like the nation at large, have come upon such extremities
of want that they are of the same mind as the Prodigal Son. Herding and
feeding with swine reminds them of their Father's home in the country
with its white bread and its fatted calf. So much is the freedom of their
faith and the purity of their morals now engaged in this return to their
Father's land of Bethlehem and Nazareth that no land proposals of the
Government should find them asleep. They must be awake and alert lest
the enemy oversow cockle in the wheat-sown field; or rob them both of
their wheat and their field.

Land-work and Hand-work

S O MANY OF OUR TOWN-DWELLERS will take their summer holiday on the land that we would encourage them to rest their weary brains not merely by a change of scene and air, but by a change of interest and thought. Doomed, as most of our town workers are doomed, to the dismal routine of office or factory, let them go out from the towns which man has made and meditate on the land as God has made it. If it can be arranged, they should go to some farmhouse, as far as possible from what we pathetically call the conveniences of modern life. I knew a great architect who, in choosing a summer dwelling place in the Cots-wolds, made it a point of necessity that there should be no railway to the nearest town.

It is best for the town-dwellers when the farm to which they go belongs to their kindred; and still better if it belongs – as many still belong, thank God! – to a good Catholic stock, for whom not a few of the conveniences of modern life are but masked inconveniences bought at a great price. In such a home and homestead there is a chance of seeing in full life some of the old hand-crafts which once made a farmhouse.

A Kingdom in Little

Much wisdom – perhaps more than might be expected of townsfolk – would be shown if these summer dwellers in the homestead could lead the same daily life as their hosts. In saying this I am not counselling the heroic, but merely suggesting to common folk the common sense of health-finding. It is the wearisome round of town-life that makes summer holidays in the country such a yearly need. But it would be good for these fugitives from town life, and in some slender degree good even for the land and the land-tillers, if their kinsfolk took a part in the daily hand-worship of the God of the hills and vales.

A man might even give his watch a rest, and time each day by the sun. The healthy, strengthening sleep bought by a day's work under the sun will come to its own natural end when the sun gently summons him through the open window to another day of fellowship in praising God. At night, whilst the hours are still young and darkness has not yet cloaked the full shoulders of the day, weariness after a day's work will be the irresistible summons to sleep.

To be afield when the earth is still sparkling with the morning's dew is to see God's earth, perhaps, as God saw it on the morning of its making. A man should make any pretence with himself or with his kin to see this miracle of jewellery in which the earth – a vain Eve, I warrant – decks and undecks herself for very joy. He should show sudden interest in the milking of the cows or the search for hidden eggs or the making of breakfast cream or the leading of cattle to their day's pasturage.

No craft in life has so many things to do as the hand-craft of wooing Nature for those her gifts which are the necessities of our life. Nor need any hour or minute be spent in merely seeking health, as, alas! it must be too often spent by...

The Poor Broken Potsherds

of our town-life. A man who, for the rest of the year, has but one little thing to do, and who is almost as broken in mind as in body because "he sees it and does it," has now each day a thousand things to choose. Whilst the grain is ripening night and day towards harvest he can take the horses to be shod, or cut back the summer effrontery of the hedges in the lane where the harvest wain must pass, or dung the byre, or, on wet days (how my fingers tingle as I write) twist straw-ropes in the barn in time for the ricks of grain, or dig potatoes in the home-garden or weed in the wheat fields, or – if, like all good farmers, he has a turn for tools – make ready the reaper, or mend the thatch, or build up fallen walls, or steep the flax in the lint-hole, or, with the farm-dog to heel, harry and shoot those thieves of rabbits in the sandy ditches near the field of oats.

None of these thousand works, that give a man the most motley day, will fail to give him time and a challenge to think. He will think all the better, and his thoughts will almost unfailingly be prayer if he is at pains to be beyond earshot or eyeshot of a daily paper. A man who has the scholarly instinct for first-hand information can hardly need a morning's paper when God has given the daily good news of daylight and the morning sun. Let him read that First (not Last) Will and Testament of his Father in Heaven, and all day long his mind will be filled with faint murmurings of the good news. Here on the land, and on the land alone, is all to be found. Everything that crowds the city shops, and makes town-life possible, must have been one day taken from the open hand of the earth. Here, and here only, nothing need go to waste: not even the leisure moments which a tired brain must have to fit it for more and more weariness of spirit. Here, and here alone, is...

The World's Cleansing Place

where all the dross of human life is given back its cradle innocence. Here, and here alone, the earth takes even the ordure of our towns and grate-fully gives us back her thanks in the harvest of autumn. Here what the earth might corrupt the air will cleanse. Here, where earth or air or water will not mend, the sun with sovereign power will touch to life. Here, and here only, when men have built Romes and Jerusalems for inevitable doom, may the nations flee as to a City of Refuge: yea, as to a very *Hôtel-Dieu* – Hostel of God – where not a tear shall fall without springing up into flower and fruit, and God, in very joy for our wisdom returned, shall once more walk amongst the corn-fields.

Industrialization of Land

I T WOULD SEEM that the real problem of the nation's land has not yet
dawned upon most of those who realize that the land is the key to
all other national problems. Most of the land-lovers with schemes
of reform look upon land reform as a matter of labourer's wage, or cheap
transit, or a minimum price, or a bounty, or plough land, or Small Holdings – or all these in one strong brew. But in their zeal for remedies which
are impressive as being First Aid of first quality they overlook the cause
of the disease, viz., the land has not been treated as land; land has been
industrialized. Land, which is the indestructible primary of economic
wealth, has been treated as if it was an economic secondary or tertiary, like
a shop or a factory. Let it be said at once that in all spheres, and especially
in that sphere of applied psychology or ethics which we call economics, to
treat a primary as if it were not a primary is to prepare chaos.

For the purposes of this short outline of the subject we may begin
by the principle that industrial or factory production is mass-production.
The machine as such seeks to justify its existence by the number of things
it can produce; so much so that the greater the production the better the
machine.

But this leads to inevitable and sometimes disastrous consequences.
Seeing that the area of production cannot consume all the product, there
must be transit to other areas of consumption. As a machine is efficient
in proportion as it multiplies production, the more perfect is the machine
the greater the production; and, in consequence, the wider must be the
area of consumption. In other words, industrial production demands an
organized and elaborate method of transit and distribution.

When a community begins the industrialization of its products,
rapid and efficient means of transit are such a good as to seem to be a
primary good. Men, and even accredited politicians and economists, like
children in a cross-channel steamer, are sometimes so fascinated by the
machinery as to lose sight of the beginning and ends of things. Railways

and motorcars, post-offices and tar-macadam roads, can be looked upon as primary wealth like wheat or butter, or a pig, or home-brewed beer, or a house. Yet all these means of rapid transit or communication might fail England tomorrow, and England of the spade and plough, England after the likeness of the thirteenth or fourteenth century, might be little the poorer, and perhaps even a little the richer, by their failure. England, shorn of its means of rapid transit and communication, might be led to see in the failure of one method of production the existence of a better. For, granted that a country is well organized when goods can be rapidly moved from the area of production to the area of consumption, yet the most efficient of all organizations is when the area of production is identical with the area of consumption. Coal hewn from the seam, raised to the pithead, carried to the city, and turned into electricity, is a most efficient motive power. But coal converted into electricity in the seam itself would be still more efficient!

It is not difficult to see the land problem in the light of these principles. Not perhaps deliberately, yet very effectively, the land of England has been gradually organized for mass production. This must not be confused with intensive production, such as may be seen here and there with or without mass production. Thus, an allotment garden on the slopes of a London railway cutting is intensive but not mass production. It grows many products, and not merely one. Moreover, these products are dominantly grown for consumption at home and not for sale in the market. But an Isle of Ely[95] small holding of orchard land is at once intensive and mass production. It grows not many products, but mainly one. Moreover, these products are grown not for consumption in the home, but for sale in the market. Such mass production as the fruit-growing round Evesham and Wisbech, the hop-growing of Kent, the potato-growing of Lincoln, and the cattle-rearing, dairy-farming, and market-garden counties of England, makes the country an agricultural factory. It is this widespread paralysis of the industrial system, and not labourers wages or lack of bounty or kindred causes that is responsible for the plight of the land. The primary degraded into a secondary has begun its inevitable revenge.

Three elements essential to industrialized or mass production are ruining the land of England: (1) the markets; (2) the transport agencies; and (3) the financiers. As soon as a land-worker produces much more of a commodity than he can consume and much fewer commodities than he must consume he must obtain money by selling his produce in a market; and the more he produces the further must he send his produce. This at once robs him of his liberty of action by delivering him to the mercy of the market, the transport agency that takes his produce to the market, and the financier who gives financial credit to buy and stock and work the land until the produce is harvested and sold and paid for. It is tragic to find the empiric verification of this principle in the letters written to the Press by farmers. These men, who know more about the agricultural than about the financial aspects of the land, complain loudly of the tyranny of Smithfield[96] or Covent Garden[97] (market), of the crushing railway rates (transport), or of the impossibility of raising wheat without a bounty so as to give a fair outlay on capital (financier). These complaints are but an empiric proof that it is folly to encourage a system which tends more and more to separate the area of production from the area of consumption; in other words, to prevent the most efficient system wherein the areas of production and consumption are identical. Moreover, these letters would seem to suggest the question whether the bounty demanded by the perplexed land-worker will not prove to be a money-grant to the markets, the railways, the financiers – i.e., to the chief causes of the farmers plight. If this is so, then the remedies suggested for the land crisis and industrial unemployment are like an effort to quench a furious fire by throwing on a few damp faggots!

Three groups of men are therefore incapable of giving the word of wisdom to England in her present land-plight: the salesman, the railway director, the financier. These men, as such, must think of their craft. But it is their craft that has brought the land to its present danger of death. They have not been wicked men; they have merely been unmitigatedly human. They have only done in their own sphere what human nature always does in its own sphere. They have seen with the eyes of their craft, aimed at the aims of their craft, toiled for the life and the supremacy of their craft. As well ask them to limit their own power, though it now be a power of destruction, as ask a paid secretary to decree the death of his own society. Smithfield and Covent Garden have aimed not at the real growth of England, but at the financial growth of Smithfield and Covent Garden. Railways have aimed not primarily at the development of England, but at the development of their traffic. High finance has sought not the real wealth of England, but the money or token-wealth of Lombard

Street.[98] They have been so successful that an acre of land in Smithfield
or Euston[99] or Lombard Street is worth a thousand acres of Sussex weald
or wold. But their success has been bought at such a price that a poet-lover
of the land has dirged:

> There is no mother in the home
> Nor ploughman in the furrow.

We have written this because we think that, although the interests
which have brought English agriculture to the point of death can see only
what they have seen, yet the men behind those interests can see the land
of England with the eyes, not of Smithfield or Euston or Lombard Street,
but of England.

P S.—Two facts, amongst thousands, may throw light on the evils
of an industrialized land.

(a) In 1923 the crop in the potato-growing lands of England was
so heavy that the town markets could not or would not buy the whole
output. Farmers could not dispose of (and still less consume) the bountiful harvest. They were therefore forced to destroy what thousands of poor
town-dwellers would have been glad to accept. But as Potatoes could not
be buried in the ground without a risk of spreading potato-disease, artificial and costly means of destroying the surplus crop had to be found!
Thus, under the system of mass production, if nature is very bountiful
(1) the farmer is in danger of heavy loss, and (2) real wealth has to be
used to destroy real wealth! This seems the *"reductio ad absurdum"* of land
industrialization,

(b) In the *Daily Mail* of October 16th, 1924, we read: "At Frank-
furt-on-Main the farmers are responsible for the disturbance. They have
not brought into the city potatoes, the chief article of food of the working classes, because they do not consider it worth the trouble to burden
themselves with more paper marks. The authorities propose to offer them
ammonia from the gas-works in exchange for potatoes." In case (a) the
Potatoes were not worth marketing on account of the breakdown of the
transport system through high freightage. In case (b) the breakdown has
occurred in the sphere of currency. In both cases there has been a dead-
lock because mass production has separated the area of production from
the area of consumption – a most perilous separation!

The return to barter (of ammonia for potatoes) is an attempt to get
in touch with the immovable base.

What Wilt Thou Have Me Do?*

THE RECENT JUDGEMENT of the Court of Appeal in the case of Stopes[100] v. Sutherland[101] is but another call to take considered action. We could have wished the judgement to be otherwise, if only for the sake of defendant, who has had to bear alone the weight of Catholic defence. Yet we shall not wish the judgement had been otherwise if the shock of the verdict opens our ears to God's call to action.

Assuredly this decision is a grievous blow to those who uphold the sanctity of family life. We may expect that the Neo-Malthusians will take advantage of the flowing tide to go forward with their successful propaganda. Public opinion will not be slow to follow legal opinion. All this will mean an intensive cannonade of the Christian family.

But we could look, if not with disinterestedness, at least with confidence on the oncoming attack if we did not see how efficiently our own surroundings are helping the enemy. Bad entrenchments are worse than no entrenchments if the enemy is alert. As our enemy has proved himself alert enough to turn defeat into victory, we can give no hostages to fortune. It is therefore our considered judgement that, however great a service this legal opinion has done to the enemy, our victory will be assured by a change not of the legal judgement, but of the state of things which has almost demanded, as it has welcomed the judgement.

To put the matter briefly. It should always he borne in mind that the Catholic Church condemns, not birth-control, but Neo-Malthusian birth-control. Physical or mechanical interference with nature's process of generation is too grievous a social hurt and too direct an incitement to sterile lust not to be a social as well as a moral evil. Yet, on the other hand, celibacy within wedlock is too abnormal a state to be counselled by wise social or moral teachers. Many of the misguided folk who are advocating sinful methods of limiting the family are sincere lovers of their fellow-

---

*Written before the final judgement of the House of Lords in favour of Dr. Sutherland.

men. If they are found to be "procurers of the Lords of Hell" it is not from any loyalty to the things of darkness, but from a mistaken idea about the path to light. Acquaintance with town problems of housing, food, clothing, and health has led them to the seemingly inevitable conclusion that if there are more children than can be provided for, the State must see that there are fewer children that shall be provided for. The production of children must not be allowed to outrun the production of the necessities of life. All this chain of reasoning is recommended by the simple formula that what is barely enough for two is not enough for three.

It need hardly be said that we do not agree with this attempt to express biological laws in mathematical formulas, as if the law of Diminishing Returns obtained only in the sphere of food-production and not also in the sphere of child-production. But with all our power and persuasiveness we would urge our Catholic leaders, cleric and lay, to ask themselves if they are trying to meet Neo-Malthusian Birth-Control in the twentieth century by those methods of mere denunciation which lost so many Catholics to the Faith in the sixteenth century.

Every careful student of the present state of our industrialized society will agree on the following two observed facts:

1. The majority of our people live not by producing and consuming things, but earning and spending a wage.

2. The modern industrial system is incapable of giving a wage sufficient for feeding, clothing, housing the normal family. Any group of Catholic Social Guildsmen can verify these facts in their own neighbourhood. They are the key to the situation, which has now ceased to be merely economic and has begun to attack the ethical foundation of the home and family.

From the latter of these two facts flow the most momentous conclusions. (a) The movement for family restriction, as such, is not a perverted sexuality. To say that it is a perverted sexuality is to disqualify the speaker as an accurate social observer. Indeed, parents of normal instincts are found to look upon family limitation not so much as a necessity for themselves as an act of charity and even of justice towards their children. Parents threatened with eviction at the birth of another child are not, manifestly, of perverted sexuality. Parents who find it impossible to house a family of eight or ten in two or three rooms are not to be dealt with merely by strident references to the doom of Onan. Indeed, they may begin to ask themselves whether extreme danger may not justify extreme measures. They may even argue that if extreme want justifies what would otherwise be theft, so does the same extreme want justify what would otherwise be lust. For the moment we leave unanswered the fallacy of this comparison. But we have stated the fallacy because it finds a show of justification in a state of things which must be met with something more practical than denunciation.

(b) It is not for the first time that we have pointed out how the present state of things offers the average parents a choice between the heroic virtue of conjugal abstinence and the mortal sin of Neo-Malthusian birth-control. We Catholics are not fulfilling our duty either to God or our neighbour merely by denouncing the sin. We must work to change the conditions which make it heroic virtue to avoid the sin. For this reason the present writer has largely lost the heart to attend congresses or summer schools on social subjects. These gatherings are happy in being a crowd of well-meaning and single-hearted men and women. But they are not happy in their avoidance of the central evil of our modern social question. They do not realize that, in the words of Pope Leo XIII, "A remedy must be found, and found quickly, for the misery and wretchedness pressing so heavily and so unjustly on the vast majority" of the hand-workers and headworkers that Neo-Malthusianism is spreading like a wild-fire. Thirty-two years have passed since these words of the Pope were uttered with prophetic warnings. Have we Catholics contented ourselves with the implicit blasphemy of saying something when we ought to have been doing something?

The Two Kings

A Meditation on Christmas Contrasts

T HE TWO KINGS are Jesus and Herod. The contrast is: on the one side, love and simplicity; on the other side, hate or indifference, or at least diplomacy. The place where these two are contrasted is either the Cave of Bethlehem or the Court of Jerusalem. In the regimental language of the captains of prayer, you can begin your meditation by making your "composition of place" either in the dark cave with the cattle, or in the brilliant court with the courtiers. Do not shirk the smell of the cattle in the Cave. It is as nothing to the Court. Besides, the Child is there with Mary, his Mother, and Joseph, his Foster-father, and all the inward scents of Heaven. This should be enough for you.

Herod is not necessarily a monster with no redeeming feature: a cruel titanic man whose strength nothing can resist.

Herod's Character

Herod was in reality a peace-loving politician with a confused desire to do the best he could for his people, and with a strong sense of royal responsibility. It has been written of him, by a modern scholar: "Herod was munificent to his friends, capable of being munificent even to his enemies.... He was a good ruler up to a point. He suppressed insurrection with absolute severity, yet never indulged in religious persecution. He was munificent to the people; when famine came he stripped his palace of gold and silver to buy corn.... He used his influence with Augustus[102] to obtain privileges for the Jews in various parts of the world.... Throughout Palestine a number of new cities were founded. (In Jerusalem) he added palaces, fortresses, parks, and pleasure grounds. But his greatest work was the reconstruction of the Temple.... Taken in his person and his career, he was one of the most conspicuous and interesting figures of his time. If he was not great, he had almost all the qualities which might have made him so" (Hastings: *Dictionary of the Bible*).

This might be the leading article on a modern Sovereign or Prime Minister, in one of the best of the tied Press. If it is not as modern as St Stephen's or Washington, it is at least a background of historic truth without which we should not realize that the Incarnation was as the Incarnate Truth.

Schemes of Reconstruction

Herod's Committee of Reconstruction had taken a statesmanlike view of their job and of their master. Town-planning schemes provided an outlet for the unemployed. Even the truculent Samaritans saw, with joy, their city Samaria turned from squalor into magnificence, due respect being paid to the historic monuments of the place. Parks sub-committees and even sanitary sub-committees were making Jerusalem into perhaps the healthiest and most artistic metropolis of the world. Moreover, the political situation of the Jewish people, in spite of the suzerainty of Rome, was in a position better than any in which it had ever been since the schism of Jeroboam. (To meditate thus on political issues is not always wrong: unless, indeed, political economy is not ethical.)

St Matthew tells us: "Then Herod, privately calling the Wise Men [i.e., the Three Kings], learned diligently of them the time of the star which appeared to them. And sending them into Bethlehem, said: Go and diligently inquire after the Child. And when you have found him, bring me word again, that I also may come and adore him" (Matt. ii 7, 8).

Herod's zeal for Infant Welfare was not demonstrably insincere. In asking these three Oriental potentates to investigate matters at Bethlehem and to make a report to him, he was acting up to the very best traditions of his class of welfare workers. Indeed, his evident sympathy with the three kings was, in embryo, a League of Nations, to be skilfully guided, no doubt, by the Big (Three plus One =) Four. The priestly class were wholeheartedly on the side of the king who was building a Temple greater than that of Solomon.

All Herod's public utterances, and indeed acts, were housed under great moral principles – Town planning, the destruction of Slumdom, the moral evils of insanitary surroundings, Child Welfare, National Prosperity, the Crime of Unemployment, International Peace, a League of Nations, the Restoration of Religion.

Satan's Plan

But – it is the special boast and business of the Evil Spirit to deceive even good men. Now, good men or weak men can be deceived only under an appearance of good. Crusades can be engineered, or at least financed, not only by heroes or saints, but by international financiers, with little concern for the Cross or the Crucified. So subtle was the plan laid by Satan for the deception, if not of King Herod, at least of the other three kings, and for the destruction of the Child King of the Jews, that an angel had to be sent to foil the skill of hell.

*****

Meanwhile, O Child King, Thou sleepest in Thy Mother's arms whilst the great world that plots Thy death under a thousand good titles lies like a hazelnut in the hollow of Thy hand. Sleep Thy child-sleep, and dream Thy child-dreams, O Babe of God, O God the Babe, lest Golgotha miss its Cross, and men their Redeemer. Thou, Prince of Peace, art scarce alighted on our soil than the sword starts from the scabbard, the blood of babes and the cry of comfortless mothers makes every hearth a place of mourning. Undo the gins and snares set for our feet by our foe and Thine; and if we dare seek a quality so divine as Peace, make our thoughts and hearts as simple as the truth, lest we add to our burden of many sins the crime of seeking evil under a plea of good. Amen.

To the Child in the Manger

A Monologue With the Son of God

"Pray for me, Father. It will be hard for me this week. I don't suppose I shall do much work this Christmas."

O Eternal Son, O Ancient of Days, these words which I speak to Thee were first spoken to me, Thy unworthy priest; and spoken, therefore, to Thee whose priest I am, though all unworthy. They burned my soul as a searing iron; because Thy servant who crooned them unto me beneath his voice was in the full winter of a long, toilsome life. His grey hairs, his halting limbs, *O Deus Fortis*, were crying to Thee for the wage of eternal life. Yet was he in want even of the wage of temporal life.

O Hidden Paradox of God who linkest extremes into Thy unutterable Unity, Thou knowest that when this my brother, whose years made him as a father, crooned his mild *miserere* to me, his father in God, I could have cried or died for grief at the mystery of his *miserere*. In Thy all-seeing, Thou dost know how baffling to my sight and understanding was this dirge of his, that "Christmas, this year, would mean no work!" Forgive my blindness of mind – or was it stubbornness of heart? – that for a moment could not understand how a man should grieve that Thy coming to the Crib should mean a lull in his daily round of toil. My soul remembers with joy what Thou didst say of Thy coming: "Come to Me, all ye that labour and are burdened, and I will refresh you." O Mystery hidden from eternity in the bosom of the Father, what great mystery is this, that Thou shouldst come amongst the poor and work-weary to rest and refresh them – and that Thy faithful servant should dread the workless days of rest and refreshment? What mystery is this, that so darkens my counsel as to add a deeper hue even to the blackness of the Cave? Lord, that I may see! Son of David, have mercy on me – that I may see.

Is it for this Thou didst become our baby brother – that we should bemoan Thy birthday as a day of wrath? Are the world's looms weaving a web so rare and fair that Thy stopping them is worthy only of a curse? Is the world's traffic so precious that to delay it even for Thee – and to make merry with Thee – is to beggar man? Is the world's work such a boon that Thou, the Riches of the Father, art as a beggar's rag? Is the world's noise music so sweet that Thou, the Word of God, the Eloquence and Poetry and Beauty of God, canst enter the world only as an interruption?

Son of David, Babe of Bethlehem, Thy servant's uncomplaining plaint to me revealed him to me; and Thee to me. Thy love for what Thou makest is so deep that not a blade of grass is reaped uncounted, and not a sparrow falls without Thy grief. The glory that was Jerusalem Thou didst account less than nought, as seeing therein the pride that built it, the covetousness that was its riches and its poverty. Outside "the Iron Gate that leadeth to the City" (Acts xii 10) didst Thou choose to be born, lest by Thy birth Thou shouldst seem to hallow what Thou camest to redeem. The hamlet of reproach, the sheepcote which David the shepherd forsook in the pride of David the king – these were Thy chosen dwelling places: their poverty Thy riches, their lowliness Thy might, their poor Thy chosen ones, their saints Thy Mother and Thy foster-father.

Such memories of dearth and war now crowd our minds that even to dream of Thee in Thy swaddling clothes must be honey-sweet. How far, alas! have we wandered from the stars and scent of Bethlehem that we should begrudge ourselves a day for remembering Thee.

O Eyes of Christ, look through the narrow doorway of Thy cave upon Thy people who, taking Thy light for darkness and Thy life for death, have strayed into a night where no life is. O Mind of Christ, give our foolishness a little of the wisdom and folly of the Crib and Cross. O Heart of Christ, break not of grief, but strengthen our hearts lest they break not of grief, but of forbidden joy.

Thou Fountain welling up into eternal life, we have drunk wells of our own digging and are sore athirst. We have turned our backs on Thee; and now, O thou who bearest the world upon Thy shoulders, our backs are bowed with the yoke of worse than Egyptian task-masters. Call us home to Thy hearth, to Thy heart, that Christmas may be again what once it was, a time of mirth when the plough shall lie still in the furrow, the hammer rest on the anvil, and only the tongue and feet of Thy children shall be busy with the song and dance!

*****

"And when he drew nigh to the house he heard music and dancing."†

---

† Luke xv 25.

The Adventure of the Land

An Open Letter to a Young Man Longing for a Life of Adventure

I TAKE IT that your ideal is not merely to seek a life of adventure such as a hunter of wild game might seek: your quest is for the adventures of a knight who risks death to befriend and rescue the weak things from the grip of the strong. You are not anxious so to live as to be rich when you die; yet you would wish to leave the world the richer by your living and your dying.

A Story With a Moral

Let me tell you a true story of England, your beloved country. Read the story tonight in your single bed-sitting-room, amidst your cheap phototypes and oleographs of cricket and football teams, and your pictures of famous boxers. Fill your whole soul with the spirit of a great game. Then, with a kiss upon the feet of your Captain, Christ, read the challenge I send out to you from my cell in N.W.5!

*****

X. was almost a derelict farm of some five hundred acre, belonging to the Duke of Z. As a means of raising a little convenient cash he sold it for about £10 an acre, or £5,000. A speculative company with no higher aim than that of making money had the intelligence to see that there was money in this waste-plot of England. They became the owners of it at £5,000.

(Here rise from your seat on the side of your bed and, pacing round and round your over-littered table – or, still better, on your knees before the image of your Captain, Christ – think on His almost cynical call to

Christian intelligence: "The children of this world are wiser in their generation than are the children of light." You will thus form the first prelude of an evening's fruitful meditation).

This company with an eye for making money divided the five hundred acres into about a hundred small holdings of three to five acres each. On each holding a cheap bungalow was built, and where needed a well was sunk. When the farm came into the hands of the company there were not a dozen human beings upon it.

An Invariable Economic Law

But the men with an eye to making money had sufficient intelligence to observe an economic law which is as invariable as the law of gravity. Land let out in small holdings is always of greater value than the same quality of land let out in large farms. In the sure hope that this law would verify itself in a few years, they sank their capital in the buying of the land, the building of bungalows, and the sinking of wells.

(Here may fitly begin the second prelude of your evening meditation. Ask yourself if you have not only as much wisdom but as much boldness as these "children of the world." Do they not shame you by the intelligence of their G.H.Q., and still more by the daring of their rank and file? Are your plans as well thought out as theirs? Is your attack as bold and dogged as theirs?)

Quickly there came to this holding of five hundred a group of land-hungry workers, husbands and wives for the most part, amongst whom were few who could be reckoned experts on the fine art of getting the most out of God's earth. Now and then there came a small market gardener or a farm hand. But the group of men who undertook the adventure of adding wealth to the England they loved included such different types as a shell-shocked joiner and an ex-detective in search of health.

From Steam-Plough to Spade

Hardly a generation has passed since this almost waste land of the Duke of Z. passed from the steam-plough to the spade. It has needed less than a generation to prove that "the spade is mightier than the plough."

X., with its five hundred acres now supporting a sturdy group of five hundred men, women, and children, would go to prove that a man needs few machines for the enriching of the earth by his toil. With such tools as he himself could make, if pressed to make – with a spade, a fork, a rough hurdle turned harrow, a log smoothed to a roller, man can give that intense garden cultivation which beggars even the harvests of virgin soil.

(Here stay your thought for a space, if only to sip and taste the truth. Summon up courage to ask yourself the difference between a *tool* and a *machine*. Is it not that the machine has but one automatic action, and the tool has almost as many actions as there are wheels and cogs in the machine? Recall the distinction which St Thomas gives when he is dealing with the theology of the Incarnate Son. He speaks of the Body of Christ as an *instrumentum conjunctum* (a personal tool), and the matter and rites of the Sacrament as an *instrumentum separatum* (a separate tool). He suggests that the highest form of tool is one which is almost identical with him who uses it, and not a machine-tool (or machine), over which a man is less a master than a caretaker and a watcher).

A Remarkable Increase

Before we left X. we tried to sum up the real wealth created by these small-holders who had fled from the token-wealth and the real poverty of English cities. Even in the eyes of that colour-blind group who measure everything by sterling the five hundred acres of derelict land have increased to four or five times their original value. I was told, to my bewilderment, that the poultry alone was valued at £10,000, or £20 an acre! Moreover, this real wealth had not been transferred by a money transaction from one part of England to another. It was not that before the transaction there were ten thousand birds at N. and ten thousand pounds it X., and that after the transaction birds and sterling had changed place. This would not be an increase, but merely a local transfer of wealth. But whereas before the transaction there was a definite number of hens, now there were ten thousand more hens in England; English brains and hands had been engaged not in mere idling but in creating *real* (as distinguished from token) wealth.

Signs of Improved Knowledge

Not only did I see in the flocks of hens and crates of eggs the sign outward and visible of this sacrament of multiplication, but I saw everywhere in this five hundred acres of England redeemed other signs of a copious redemption. Men who had little knowledge of building beyond an elementary grasp of the law of gravity had set stones upon stones for the making of a wall to shelter peaches or a sty to house pigs. There were wonderful contrivances of panelled and latticed wood called rabbit hatches. There was one noble greenhouse built by the small-holder and the local joiner at one-fourth the factory cost.

One lad I talked with as we stood beside the wealth and loveliness of three thousand eggs was proud to tell me that the bacon I had eaten that morning for breakfast was of his rearing and curing. The same lad had discovered stones in the subsoil of his father's holding, had dug them up, had wrought them into a wall to shelter peaches, and had reached the seventh heaven when his father had said he was glad to use the miniature quarry-hole as a tank for rain-water!

(Here kneel down and make a litany of the things God has given to your keeping and as the conditions of your adventure. Say slowly such noble words as air, fire, clay, soil, rain, snow, hail, wind, south-west, hay, corn, oats, stubble, stone, brick, lime, spade, fork, rake— But oh! to think that here in N.W. 5 many of these ultimates of human life and energy and beauty are but dim memories or tear-dimmed regrets— I cannot go on, for the loneliness that is in my heart! But you are young, O my brother, and you may one day tread the land which I can but discern afar off in the clouds that reveal the rising of the sun).

Notes.

[1] *Rerum Novarum*, or "The Workers Charter," was issued by Pope Leo XIII on May 15, 1891, and was sub-titled "On the Condition of the Working Classes." The reason for the Encyclical was expressed therein as follows: "That the spirit of revolutionary change, which has long been disturbing the nations of the world, should have passed beyond the sphere of politics and made its influence felt in the cognate sphere of practical economics is not surprising. The elements of the conflict now raging are unmistakable...in the changed relations between masters and workmen; in the enormous fortunes of some few individuals, and the utter poverty of the masses." In order words, the encyclical sought to address, from a Catholic perspective, the problem of Capitalism and the false "remedy" of Socialism which is its rebellious offspring.

[2] Babylon. According to the *Oxford Companion to the Bible*, "the rendering of Akkadian Babilum, the city that for centuries served as capital of the land of Babylon." It is the location of the "tower of Babel" to be founded mentioned in Genesis, and is the area covered by modern-day Iraq.

[3] St. Pancras. A borough of central London, north of the River Thames.

[4] *Dieu le veut.* "God so wishes it."

[5] *Fiat.* "Let it be so."

[6] *The Times.* London daily newspaper founded by John Walter I (1739–1812) as the *Daily Universal Register* on January 1, 1785; it became *The Times* on May 18, 1788.

[7] George Lansbury (1859–1940). Grew up in the poverty of London's East End, and became a Socialist MP for the area in 1910. Shortly before World War I, he became Editor of the Labour paper, *The Daily Herald*, through the pages of which his fervent pacifism appeared. He went to prison in 1921, along with 29 other Labour councillors in London, for refusing to levy rates upon the poor. He was the leader of the Labour Party from 1931 to 1935. At the time of his death, he was the President of the Peace Pledge Union.

[8] Poplar. An area of East London on the north bank of the River Thames.

[9] NW5. Zone of London indicated by its direction and distance from the center of the city. London, both inner and outer, is divided into zones which are designated by letters and by numbers, indicating, respectively, the direction ("N.W." signifying North West, for instance) and relative distance from the city center.

[10] *Maranatha.* Literally, "the Lord is come." When appended to the "anathema" it becomes a very solemn formula, similar to but much stronger than the simple *anathema*, by which the criminal is excommunicated, abandoned to the judgment of God, and rejected from the bosom of the Church until the coming of the Lord (from the *Catholic Encyclopedia*, 1908).

[11] Euclid of Alexandria (c325BC–265BC). The most prominent of the mathematicians of Antiquity. He is best known for his treatise, *The Elements*, in which he demonstrates geometric axioms by assuming the contrary of the axiom he intends to prove, and showing that such assumptions lead to absurdities. Thus Fr. McNabb's citation of him.

[12] 5s. "Five shillings," "s" being the abbreviation for a shilling. Under the system of pre-decimal Imperial currency then in circulation, there were 20 shillings in a pound, and each shilling was equivalent to 12 pence (the plural of penny), abbreviated by "d." Thus 5d. would mean five pence.

[13] Waterloo. A reference to the battle which took place on June 18, 1815, in what is now part of the Netherlands. Following the return of Napoleon Bonaparte to Paris from exile on the Island of Elba in March of 1815 with a large and growing army, the Congress of Vienna decided that he had to be defeated on the battlefield. The Duke of Wellington, in command of Belgian, Dutch, and British forces possessed an army of some 67,000 troops, whilst his ally, Marshal Blucher, headed a Prussian army of some 52,000. Napoleon, with some 72,000 troops at his disposal, was defeated.

[14] Robert Stewart, Lord Castlereagh (1769–1822). Son of the Marquis of Londonderry, he was elected to the Irish Parliament in 1790, and to Westminster in 1794. Having entered politics as a Whig, he quickly joined the Tories under William Pitt, who gave him the Castlereagh title. He played a key role in the suppression of the Irish revolt of 1798. Both Pitt and he believed that the only way to quell social unrest in both England and Ireland was to unite the countries under one Parliament; as a result, the Act of Union took place in 1801. In 1817, following the Napoleonic war, unemployment and social unrest rose rapidly in England, leading to clashes between radical reformers and government troops, such as occurred in 1819 at the Peterloo massacre. Castlereagh sought to alleviate the situation by suspending *Habeas Corpus* – the right of citizens to ensure that they are not illegally imprisoned – and enacted the "Six Acts" in 1819. Instead of quelling the situation, the Acts exacerbated it as a result of their suppression of popular rights and freedoms. In consequence, Castlereagh's popularity plunged, which ultimately led to his suicide.

[15] John Lawrence Hammond (1872–1949). He was the Editor of *The Speaker* between 1899 and 1906. After WWI, he went to work for the *Manchester Guardian*. He wrote a number of books in co-operation with his wife – Lucy Barbara Bradby (1873–1961) – about the impact of the Industrial Revolution on the working classes. In addition to the book cited by Fr. McNabb, they wrote *The Village Labourer* (1911) and *The Town Labourer* (1917).

[16] *The Political Register.* Newspaper founded by William Cobbett (1763–1835) in 1802, and which ran to 88 volumes by the time it ceased publication in 1835. It

provided a radical critique of the evils and influence of Capitalism in English society, and was the main paper read by the working class.

[17] William Lamb, Lord Melbourne (1779–1848). A barrister who entered Parliament in 1806 and became Chief Secretary of Ireland in 1827. He was twice Prime Minister, once in 1834, and again from 1835 to 1841.

[18] Richard Brinsley Sheridan (1751–1816). Playwright who, along with his father-in-law, managed to buy the celebrated Drury Lane Theatre in London in 1776. However that very year, Sheridan met Charles Fox (1749–1806), the radical Whig politician, and decided to enter politics. He entered Parliament in 1780, remaining faithful to Fox's views until the end, and joined the 1783 government of William Pitt. Sheridan was regarded as a powerful orator.

[19] *The Masque of Anarchy.* Poem by Percy Shelley (1792–1822) written following the 1819 Peterloo Massacre. Henry Addington, Lord Sidmouth (1759–1844) entered Parliament in 1784, becoming Speaker of the House of Commons in 1789. He was Prime Minister from 1801 to 1804, and was ennobled in 1805. A member of Lord Liverpool's government in 1812, he sought to deal with social unrest through suppression and execution, and he was especially hard on the Luddites. He voted against the Catholic Emancipation Act in 1829 and against the Reform Act of 1832. John Scott, Lord Eldon (1751–1838) was a major political and legal figure during the reigns of George III and George IV – and even into the early reign of Queen Victoria. He entered Parliament in the 1780s, becoming Lord Eldon in 1799. He was Lord Chancellor from 1801 to 1821.

[20] Finn MacColl. Finn Mac Cumhal, the last and greatest leader of the Fianna, the famous warrior people of Irish mythology.

[21] Possibly a reference to Sir Charles Cameron (1841–1924). Entered Parliament in 1874 and served almost 24 years. He introduced the Inebriates Act in 1898, and became an Honorary Freeman of the City of Dublin in 1911.

[22] *Non licet esse vos.* "Your existence is not licit." The Roman juridical formula regarding Christians and Christianity following in the wake of the anti-Christian persecutions under Emperor Nero, and which inspired the legislation during the succeeding epoch.

[23] *Morning Post.* Daily newspaper founded in 1772. Initially employed notable writers such as Samuel Coleridge, Robert Southey, William Wordsworth and Charles Lamb to improve its status and circulation. Purchased by Sir James Berry, owner of the *Daily Telegraph,* a paper founded in 1855, and still being published; contrary to Berry's original intentions, the two papers were quickly amalgamated.

[24] Clerkenwell. An area of East-Central London on the north bank of the River Thames.

[25] Shoreditch. Another area of East London on the north bank of the River Thames.

[26] Whig. The Whigs of the early 19th century were the predecessors of the reform-minded Liberals who grouped themselves around William Gladstone, first Prime Minister of England in 1868. They had their origins in the party of those who opposed Charles II in the run-up to the so-called Glorious Revolution of 1688 – which was brought about by a cabal of the richest magnates in the England of the day, and who aimed at subordinating (and successfully so) the power of the Crown to Parliament, which they controlled.

[27] Tory. Nowadays simply a supporter of the British Conservative Party; but in its origins the word refers to those who opposed the exclusion of James II, supported the Stuart claim after the so-called Glorious Revolution of 1688–89, but accepted the established order in Church and State during the reign of George III in 1760. The root of the word "Tory" comes from the Gaelic for "outlaw," or to "pursue" – *tóir.*

[28] Lambeth. An area of south central London, on the south bank of the River Thames.

[29] In modern editions of what is now known to be St. Thomas's *De Regno*, this is Chapter VII of Book II.

[30] In St. Thomas's original, this is a reference to the famous Roman architect, Marcus Vitruvius Pollio (c90-20BC), who had a great admiration for Greek architecture, and wrote *De Architectura*, which, in ten books, deals with city planning and architecture in general, building materials, temple construction, public and private buildings, clocks, hydraulics, and civil and military engines. It is in Book II of his work that he relates the story of Dinocrates (*vide infra*) and Alexander.

[31] In the original *De Regno*, the reference here is to Dinocrates, a Macedonian architect employed by Alexander in the building of Alexandria in Egypt, from 332 to 331B.C.

[32] Alexander the Macedonian (356BC–323BC). Better known in history as Alexander the Great. He became King of Macedonia in 336, and launched his campaign in 334 to punish the Persians for their previous invasion of Greece. His campaign took him to Persia, Syria, Egypt, Afghanistan and India. Major victories were had at Chaeronea (338), Tyre (332) and Megalopolis (331). He died preparing an invasion of Arabia.

[33] Probably a reference to the tale of Barlaam and Josephat, a legend of Christian antiquity originating in India, and detailing Josephat's conversion to Christianity by the holy hermit Barlamm, despite the best efforts of Josephat's father, King Abenner, who persecuted the Indian Christian Church in the third or fourth century.

[34] *De te fabula narratur.* From the longer *"Quid rides? Mutato nominee de te fabula narratur"* ("Why laugh? Change the names and the story would apply to you"), from the *Satires* of Horace, Book I, 1, 69–70.

[35] *Ipsi viderimus.* "We will see."

[36] *New Witness.* Weekly political journal founded in 1912; successor to the *Eye Witness* founded by Belloc in 1911 and edited jointly by him and Cecil Chesterton. Dedicated to exposing corruption in government, it ceased publication in 1912, at which point Chesterton purchased it, renamed it the *New Witness*, and invited his friend, Ada Jones, to become his editorial assistant. When Chesterton enlisted in 1916, his brother, G.K., took over the paper. In 1925 it became *G.K.'s Weekly*, which G.K. continued to edit until his death in 1936.

[37] Archbishop Richard Chevenix Trench (1807–1886). An English philologist, theologian and poet, who was also the Anglican Archbishop of Dublin. McNabb's reference stems from the fact that Trench criticized the English language dictionaries available in 1857. He pointed out that they were merely versions of Samuel Johnson's two volume dictionary published in 1757, and which contained a mere 40,000 definitions. He expressed the view that English clearly had far more words than that. He was innovative in that he called for a dictionary that contained *every* word with *every* sense and with *every* meaning; furthermore he demanded that such dictionaries carry illustrative quotations so as to show the context of every word. In other words, the modern dictionary is a consequence of Trench's radical critique.

[38] Funk & Wagnalls. American publishers of Dictionaries and Encyclopediae.

[39] A reference to Plato's comment in book IV of his *Republic* that "the music and literature of a country cannot be altered without major political and social changes." Plato (427BC–347BC) was an important Greek philosopher who began as a student under Socrates, following whose death, he went to Egypt to study under the students of Pythagoras. Returning to Greece, Plato founded his own School at the Academy. His works include *The Republic, Timaeus, The Laws*, and numerous others.

[40] General William Booth (1829–1892). Started out as a preacher for Wesleyan Methodism, and was thus sent to the Methodist New Connexion Church in London in 1852. In 1861, however, he set up his own evangelistic operation which became the "Christian Mission" in Whitechapel, London, in 1865. By 1878, it had transformed itself into the Salvation Army, which was notable for its military style uniforms and the use of military hierarchy. A remarkable organizer, Booth traveled widely spreading his message. In 1890, he wrote *In Darkest England and the Way Out*.

[41] Joseph Robert Clynes (1869–1949). Self-educated man who helped to found the Piercers Union in 1886. Became a full- time union organizer in 1892, and

entered Parliament as a Socialist MP in 1906. A talented writer, he contributed regularly to papers such as Robert Blatchford's *Clarion.* Became the leader of the Parliamentary Labour Party in 1910, and Home Secretary in MacDonald's government in 1929.

[42] Dick Turpin (1705–1739). Born John Palmer, he was a thief and petty criminal who gradually worked his way up in the criminal world in southern England. He became a highwayman and drew sufficient attention to himself that King George offered £50 for his capture. When Palmer met "Captain" Tom King, the most famous of the highwaymen of the day, "Dick Turpin" was born. Eventually Palmer ended up murdering two people in different circumstances. In 1737, he moved to northern England, setting himself up as a country gentleman. He financed his new lifestyle through horse and cattle rustling. Hanged for murder, he was a far cry from his popular legend of being a daring and dashing highwayman.

[43] *Delerium tremens.* Literally, "trembling delirium." Usually refers to symptoms suffered due to withdrawal resulting from the cessation of chronic consumption of alcohol.

[44] Tube. The English term for "subway."

[45] Admiral John Arbuthnot Fisher (1841–1920). Becoming a Captain at just 33, he is generally believed to be the finest Admiral since Nelson in the English Fleet. After seeing much active war service, he was promoted to Third Sea Lord at the British Admiralty in 1892. An unconventional man, he turned up on his first day at the Admiralty with a placard around his name saying: "I have no work to do!" Made First Sea Lord in 1904, he was a great modernizer of the Fleet and he made great progress in a few short years, hence his reputation for scrapping obsolete naval vessels. Became Baron Fisher of Kilverstone in 1909.

[46] County Galway is located on the western coast of Ireland and is part of the province of Connaught.

[47] William Cobbett (1766–1835). Born to poor parents in Hampshire in England, he rose to become one of the most famous polemical journalists of his day, his reputation being based on his fearlessness and his profound integrity. At a time when Catholics were still being persecuted in England, he found the courage to write that "the Protestant religion had been established by gibbets, racks and ripping knives," though Cobbett himself was *not* Catholic.

[48] David Lloyd George (1863–1946). Entered Parliament as a Liberal Member in 1890. Served in various government posts, notably as Chancellor of the Exchequer under Herbert Asquith from 1908 to 1915. Became Prime Minister in 1916 after striking a deal with Conservatives to oust Asquith; he remained in the post until his resignation in 1922. He continued to lead the Liberal party for a number of years.

[49] The Cotswolds are a range of hills to be found in Gloucestershire, in the West of England.

[50] *Beato Angelico* – "the Blessed Angelico." A reference to Guido di Pietro, better known as Fra Angelico (1400–1485). A Dominican monk and Florentine painter, he spent most of his life in S. Domenico in Fiesole, becoming its Prior in 1450, but he traveled extensively for his prestigious commissions. The private chapel of Pope Nicolas V in the Vatican was frescoed with "Scenes from the Lives of SS. Stephen and Lawrence" between 1447 and 1450. Although known as *Beato Angelico* for centuries, he was only officially beatified in 1984.

[51] Bayswater is an area of the West End of London, and Kilburn is an area of northwest London, both on the north bank of the River Thames. Rotherhithe is an area of southeast London on the south bank of the River Thames.

[52] *Timeo Danaos.* From the longer, *"timeo Danaos et dona ferentes"* ("I fear Greeks, even when they offer gifts"), from the *Aeneid* of Virgil, Book II, 48.

[53] St. Thomas Aquinas (1225–1274). The official Philosopher of the Catholic Church. His first Summa was the *Summa of Christian Teaching*, which was prepared specially to deal with those who did not have the Catholic faith: pagans, Jews, Greek schismatics and Muslims. His second, begun in 1266, was the *Summa Theologica* for which he is most famous, and which was a beginner's (!) introduction to Catholic theology. Mary Clarke, the Thomist writer, says: "To know St. Thomas is to know the medieval mind at its finest, its most powerful, and, indeed, its most modern. For he is timeless and timely, a man for all ages."

[54] Hammurabi was the sixth king of the Amorite Dynasty that settled in Babylon between 1894BC and ended around 1595BC. During his long reign (1792–1750BC), local governors referred many problems to him, with the result that towards the end of his life he drew up his now famous Code. It is a series of regulations for various circumstances, rather than a comprehensive body of law, and it is written in casuistic form: "If a man does...then..." The penalties were graded according to the social status of the injured party.

[55] Francis Galton (1822–1911). A British psychologist and evolutionist who was a pioneer in the development of Biometry (the science of the application of statistical methods to biological facts) and the founder of Eugenics, the "science" of hereditary improvement.

[56] Tyre and Sidon. Cities on the southern coast of Lebanon, which were ancient commercial and shipping centers, dating from the second millennium, B.C.

[57] Nineveh. One of the most ancient cities of Assyria, and its capital from the seventh century B.C. It was located in what is now northeastern Iraq.

[58] From §36 of the "Program of Social Reconstruction," issued by the Administrative Committee of the National Catholic War Council, February 12, 1919.

[59] *Ibid.,* §40.

[60] Whitechapel. An area of the East End of London, on the north bank of the River Thames.

[61] Lord William George Armstrong (1810–1900). Engineer, industrialist, and philanthropist, who developed the hydraulic crane, the Armstrong gun, and founded Elswick Works shipbuilding. Also founded and contributed to many charitable causes.

[62] British Association. A reference to the British Association for the Advancement of Science, founded in 1831 to strengthen the relationship between science and the public interest. Included a department dedicated to economic and social problems founded in 1833 principally by Charles Babbage, Thomas Malthus and Adam Sidgwick, and variously referred to as "Section F," the "Statistical Section," and the "Economic Section."

[63] Alfred Arthur Hopkinson (1879–1962). Industrialist, inventor, and Member of Parliament for Mossley from 1918 to 1929 and again from 1931 to 1945.

[64] A.A. Mitchell. Scholar who also contributed articles to the *Proceedings of the Royal Philosophical Society of Glasgow*, "Nationalization," February 16, 1921, and "Unemployment," January 23, 1924.

[65] Charles Bathhurst, Lord Bledisloe (1867–1958). The Earls of the Bathhurst family have maintained their seat at Cirencester in England since 1690. Charles entered Parliament in 1910, holding in the course of his career many government positions. He was appointed to the Privy Council in 1926, and was Governor-General of New Zealand from 1929 to 1935.

[66] Adam W. Kirkcaldy. Professor of Economics, University College, Nottingham, and scholar associated with "Section F" of the British Association, during the first part of the 20th century. Author of several books, including *Economics and Syndicalism* (1914), and *British Finance During and After the War, 1914-21* (1921).

[67] *The Catholic Times.* Originally founded as *The Northern Press* in 1867 by English Catholic priest, temperance advocate, apologist, and social reformer, James Nugent (1822–1905). His paper became *The Catholic Times* in March of 1872. It is currently published as a weekly companion to *The Universe.*

[68] Lindisfarne. An island off the coast of England, in Northumbria, just south of the English-Scottish border, called the "Holy Island" for its rich religious history. In 635 St. Aidan founded a monastery there, having been granted the land by St. Oswald, King of Northumbria. St. Cuthbert arrived at Linsidfarne in 651, three years after St. Aidan's death, and became the Bishop there in 684.

[69] Dr. C. Killick Millard (1871–1952). Leicester Medical Officer of Health who advocated euthanasia and birth control. Founded the Voluntary Euthanasia Legalization Society (later called the Euthanasia Society) in 1936; President of the Leicester Rotary Club from 1940 to 1941. Wrote *Euthanasia: A Plea for the*

Legalisation of Voluntary Euthanasia under Certain Conditions in 1931.

[70] The Rotary Club. Founded in 1905 by Percy Harris in Chicago. By 1969, it had some 13,500 clubs around the world. A sub-division is *Rotaract*, which is for young people between 17 and 25 years of age, whilst the *Inner Wheel* is for the wives of Rotarians. In the Club's prospectus it says "its conception of service to humanity in all its forms is in harmony with all religions, and exercises no political influence." Before Vatican II, the Catholic Church attacked entities like the Rotary Club as White Freemasonry, i.e., organizations which promoted Masonic ideals, and especially false humanism and religious indifference.

[71] Sir George Newman (1870–1948). Public health pioneer in England, who served variously as County Medical Officer for Bedfordshire and Medical Officer of Health for Finsbury; first Chief Medical Officer of the medical department of the British Board of Education, and the first Chief Medical Officer of the British Ministry of Health from 1919 to 1935.

[72] Phidias (c. 490–430BC). Generally regarded as the greatest of the sculptors of ancient Greece, who lived during its "Golden Age," and worked both in bronze and in ivory and gold. His first known commission was from Pericles, to execute a bronze monument to General Miltiades (the hero of the battle of Marathon) and other national heroes. He supervised construction of the Parthenon, and contributed to it a number of statues, including the famous statue of Athena. He also created such famous monuments as the massive sculpture of Zeus at Olympia.

[73] St. Augustine of Hippo (354–430). One of the greatest Christian thinkers of antiquity, and a Doctor of the Catholic Church. His genius was to fuse the valuable knowledge of the classical world with Christian doctrine. His *Confessions* and *The City of God* are his foremost works.

[74] Dr. J.H. Clapham (1873–1946). A well-known historian at King's College, Cambridge. His first book was *The Woollen and Worsted Industries* (1907), which was to be followed by *The Economic History of Modern Britain* (1926), *The Economic Development of France and Germany 1815–1914* (1928) and *The Bank of England: A History* (1944).

[75] The Report of the Provisional Joint Committee presented to a meeting of the Industrial Conference. A report of a committee of representatives of employers and trades unions commissioned by the British Industrial Conference to deal with working hours, wages, and conditions, and unemployment, and delivered to the Conference in Westminster on April 4, 1920.

[76] Sir Allan Smith. Scottish MP and business leader; variously chairman of the general purposes committee of the British Empire Union; member of the 1919 Royal Commission on Coal and, later, the Balfour Commission on Trade and Industry; and secretary of the Engineering Employers Federation.

[77] Arthur Henderson (1863–1935). Issue of poor Scottish family, he was an official with the Iron Founders Union. Entered Parliament in 1903 and became Chairman of the Parliamentary Labour Party. Was responsible for bringing about British diplomatic recognition of Soviet Russia. Awarded the Nobel Prize for Peace in 1934.

[78] Whitley Report. In October of 1916, the British Government established a committee under the direction of J.H. Whitley, MP (1866–1935), then Speaker of the House of Commons, to investigate relations between employers and laborers. His report, completed after three years of study, recommended the establishment of Joint Industrial Councils (later nicknamed "Whitley Councils") to deal with wages, working conditions, unemployment, and labor-management relations.

[79] Cardinal Francis Bourne (1861–1935). Entered the priesthood in 1884 and became the Bishop of Southwark, London, in 1897. He became the Archbishop of Westminster in 1903 and received the cardinalate in 1911.He was a mild man who sought to advance the Catholic Church in England through patient understanding of the "sensibilities" of the British government, though he believed wholeheartedly that there was nothing more native to England than Catholicism.

[80] Lanfranc (c1005–1089). An Italian churchman and theologian who taught the future St. Anselm. Made Archbishop of Canterbury by William the Conqueror. He was also a Benedictine monk who maintained good relations between the King and the Papacy and reformed the English Church. His work, *De Corpore et Sanguine Domine*, had a strong resonance in medieval theology.

[81] St. Thomas à Becket (1118?–1170). Appointed Lord Chancellor to Henry II of England (reigned 1154–1189) in 1154. A Cistercian, he was ordained on June 2, 1162, and consecrated a bishop the following day. From thereon, he was in constant tension with the King, who sought, as Thomas saw it, the aggrandizement of the Kingdom at the expense of the real interests of the Church; meanwhile, Becket maintained, to safeguard the Church's independence, that clergy charged with criminal offenses should not be subject to the jurisdiction of civil courts but should be tried and punished by Church authorities only. When confronted by four knights who had come to kill him – whether at Henry's bidding or not is not clear – they asked "Where is the traitor?" to which he replied: "Here I am, no traitor, but archbishop and priest of God." Killed in his own church, devotion to him spread so quickly that by 1173 he was canonized by the Pope. In 1174, Henry II did public penance, being scourged at St. Thomas's tomb.

[82] Wisbech St Mary's. A small market town in Cambridgeshire in East Anglia.

[83] Thomas Babington, Lord Macaulay (1800–1859). Although he trained as a

lawyer, he spent most of his life in politics, having entered Parliament in 1830. He was a good orator who was passionately anti-slavery and achieved some notable successes in that field. He retired to write his five-volume *History of England* (published between 1848 and 1855), which was subsequently translated into over a dozen languages. Whilst his literary style is not in question, his grasp of "history" is, since the whole of England's past is evaluated by reference to Britain's mid-19th-century constitution. Nevertheless, there is certain merit in the passage to which Fr. McNabb alludes, which was written by Macaulay in his 1840 review of Leopold von Ranke's *The Ecclesiastical and Political History of the Popes during the Sixteenth and Seventeenth Centuries* (London, 1840), and included in Volume II of his *Critical and Historical Essays* (1843). The entire phrase is:

> She [the Roman Catholic Church] may still exist in undiminished vigour when some traveller from New Zealand shall, in the midst of a vast solitude, take his stand on a broken arch of London Bridge to sketch the ruins of St. Paul's.

[84] Sir Richard Arkwright (1732–1792). English inventor whose inventions and organization contributed to the beginning of the Industrial Revolution and its factory system.

[85] George Stephenson (1781–1848). Self-taught enginewright who created his first locomotive, *Blutcher*, in 1814. An innovative and far-seeing engineer who moved steadily up the career ladder, becoming the Chief Engineer of the Stockton and Darlington Company in 1821. He created the first railway locomotive, *Locomotion*, in 1825, and subsequently contributed immensely to the development of the railway system in England.

[86] Sir Charles Algernon Parsons (1854–1931). Widely regarded as one of the most gifted of British engineers. He built the first multi-stage reaction turbine in 1884. In the same period, he began experimenting on marine steam turbines, producing the *Turbinia* in 1894 which could sail at 30 knots.

[87] John Ruskin (1819–1900). Artist, scientist, poet, philosopher and art critic. He helped the Pre-Raphaelites to establish their reputation through his written interventions, and did much to support artists such as Rossetti, Millais and Holman Hunt.

[88] Ealing, Camden Town, Paddington, Westbourne Grove. All areas of London covering the west and northwest, and all located on the north bank of the River Thames.

[89] G.K. Chesterton (1874–1936). Although he dismissed himself as a mere journalist, he was, in fact, a novelist, a socio-economic theoretician and a profound lay theologian. Legouis & Cazamian in their *History of English Literature* describe him as "the champion of orthodoxy. To this word he has given a more and more substantial meaning."

[90] Hilaire Belloc (1870–1953). Poet, novelist, critic, essayist and controversial-

ist. A close friend of Chesterton, Legouis & Cazamian say of him: "Belloc's paradoxes are more careful than those of Chesterton; his manner is freer from tricks; while he has not the same vigour, he possesses a more varied and surer charm of expression."

[91] Dr. O'Hara. Probably a reference to Archbishop Edwin Vincent O'Hara (1881–1956), who in 1923 organized the National Catholic Rural Life Conference in 1923, for the vindication and defense of the rural and agrarian life as the backbone of society and the Church, the addressing of the pastoral needs of rural Catholics, and the defense of the small, family farm from business and industrial interests.

[92] St. Dominic's Press. A Distributist publishing endeavor located in the village of Ditching in East Sussex, eight miles north of Brighton. Founded in 1915 by Hilary Pepler – who was also a magnificent puppeteer –as part of the community encouraged by Fr. McNabb to show the way forward for craftsmen, rural enthusiasts, and Catholics. The Press printed many of Eric Gill's books, and specialized in Catholic devotional books and Mass cards.

[93] Victor Alexander John Hope, the Second Marquis of Linlithgow (1887–1952). Conservative British statesman who served in numerous government posts, including Civil Lord of the Admiralty (1922–1924) and Deputy Chairman of the Unionist Party Organisation (1924–1926), prior to his appointment as Viceroy of India (1936–1943). He was very interested in agriculture, and chaired the departmental committee on the distribution and prices of agricultural produce in 1923, from which proceeded the report referred to by Fr. McNabb.

[94] *Ca'canny.* A Scottish expression which literally means "go slow" or "be careful not to do too much," and was employed by some leaders of industrial unionism during the last part of the 19th century to imply a strike accomplished, while remaining on the payroll, by a slackening of workmen's efficiency and performance, in order to cost industrial owners and management profits, and in an attempt to wring from them higher wages.

[95] The Isle of Ely. A small market town in East Anglia, northeast of the city of Cambridge.

[96] Smithfield Market. One of the oldest markets in London, established in 1174. It is largely known for the selling of meat, though it now also sells dairy products. The City of London was granted a Charter by Edward III in 1327 for the market, though today it is owned by the Corporation of London.

[97] Covent Garden. A market on the north bank of the River Thames which specializes in selling fruit and vegetables. It was London's first piazza, having been commissioned in 1630 by the fourth Earl of Bedford, who gave the work of design to Inigo Jones. Today, it is a complex of shops and cafés that hosts street theatre and entertainment.

[98] Lombard Street. A street in east-central London, known for banking, investment and all that pertains to money. Sometimes considered the "Wall Street" of the 19th Century.

[99] Euston. A small area of central London in the Bloomsbury district of the city, known for its elegant architecture and cultural history.

[100] Marie Stopes (1880–1958). The founder of what is now the *International Marie Stopes Clinic* network which purports to promote "Family Planning." In 1905, she was Britain's youngest Doctor of Science. Her first book, *Married Love*, was about marriage and feminism, although by then her first marriage had been annulled on the grounds of non-consummation! The book was, notably, banned in the USA as "obscene." When Margaret Sanger, an American Socialist who promoted birth control and abortion, had to flee America in 1915, she teamed up with Marie Stopes. In 1918, Stopes wrote *Wise Parenthood* which outraged both the Church of England and the Catholic Church in England since both were opposed to contraception. In 1921, Stopes – described by one adulatory source as "the twentieth century advocate of sexual pleasure" – founded the *Society for Constructive Birth Control* as well as the first "family planning" clinic in Holloway, London. One aspect usually passed over by "fans" these days is that she was a fanatical eugenist – to the point that she disowned her own child for her choice of marriage partner.

[101] Dr. Halliday Sutherland. A leading Catholic apologist and doctor who wrote a book entitled *Birth Control* (1923) in which he described Stopes's work on the subject as obscene, for which description Stopes sued him for libel. As Fr. McNabb indicates, Stopes won the first round in court, but the judgment was eventually overturned by the House of Lords. In 1935, Dr. Sutherland wrote *The Laws of Life* which was described in the Irish Senate by Professor Magennis as "a medical book of extreme value to medical practitioners and to priests as confessors."

[102] Caesar Augustus (31BC–14AD). The Roman Emperor who, through diligent effort and military and political campaigns, brought an end to the decline of the Roman Republic through the establishment of the Principate which, in spite of its flaws, gave Rome three centuries of relative peace, prosperity and stability.

Some Thoughts on Reading Fr. McNabb
by William Fahey

R eaders unfamiliar with McNabb will wish to read selectively, intelligently. Begin with his first essay (always a fine launching point), from there seek out those topics that seem immediately appealing, conclude with the final essay and perhaps an ale. As a man of flesh and blood, McNabb was rooted in a specific place and time, and possessed of his own interests. Thus, certain essays may befuddle those not cognizant of every twist and turn in early-twentieth-century British political life. Yet *because* McNabb was a man rooted in a place and time, he could stand firm and fix his gaze on the heavens. He was not a nomad, though he may rescue those orphaned by nomadic Progress. He remains a great guide for the intrepid and receptive soul.

For those whose interest has been piqued, there are various ways to continue. First, become acquainted with the man and his Age. An excellent starting point remains the only published biography, that of fellow Dominican Ferdinand Valentine, *Father Vincent McNabb, O.P.: The Portrait of a Great Dominican* (The Newman Press, 1955). For moving, but only loosely connected vignettes, E.A. Siderman's *A Saint in Hyde Park: Memories of Father Vincent McNabb, O.P.* (The Newman Press, 1950) presents an inspiring picture. And the special issue of *The Chesterton Review*, vol. 22.1-2, dedicated to McNabb, is well worth the hunt.

Better than reading *about* McNabb, one should *read* McNabb. This will demand provisions and an adventurous spirit, for little is now in print – the reader is thereby presented with a fine opportunity for scouring second-hand book shops. Beware: McNabb appears in religion, devotion, biography, politics, economics, and *belles lettres.* A good sampling of his work was put together by Francis Edward Nugent and entitled a *Father McNabb Reader* (P.J. Kennedy & Sons, 1954). Of McNabb's devotional writing, the most immediately rewarding remain *Stars of Comfort* (Henry Regnery Company, 1958) and *The Craft of Prayer* (Newman Press, 1951). Of his literary and social criticism, consider *From a Friar's Cell* (P.J. Kennedy & Son, 1924), *Old Principles and the New Order* (Sheed & Ward, 1942), and, of course, *The Church and the Land*. Sadly, many gems of McNabb's thought lie buried only in the pages of numerous academic journals and newspapers to which he was a regular contributor.

What made a McNabb? I would suggest that the tradition which he exemplified starts in the Prophetic books of the Old Testament, Hesiod's *Works & Days*, Virgil's *Georgics*, the fiery writings of St. Patrick, the *Rule* of St. Benedict, and the preaching and treatises of St. Dominic and, emphatically, St. Thomas Aquinas. An excellent overview of this latter Dominican tradition and its relationship to social concerns may be found in George H. Speltz, *The Importance of Rural Life According to the Philosophy of St. Thomas Aquinas* (Washington, D.C., 1945; reprinted Wipf and Stock Publishers, 2003). Speltz, it should be noted, went on to become a bishop and an important figure in the Catholic Rural Life Movement in the United States.

In the British tradition, McNabb reminds one of William Cobbett, the founding father – in many respects – of the British critique of Industrialism and Capitalism. The French tradition, which would have been influential on McNabb and his circle through the research of Belloc and Dawson, has been anthologized and recently translated by Christopher Olaf Blum in his *Critics of the Enlightenment: Readings in the French Counter-Revolutionary Tradition* (Intercollegiate Studies Institute, 2003).

Finally, in the Catholic social teaching tradition, McNabb was informed principally by the encyclicals of Leo XIII. Two particularly useful anthologies of these writings are *Social Wellsprings: Fourteen Epochal Documents by Leo XIII*, ed. J. Husslein, S.J. (Bruce, 1940) and *The Church and Labor*, ed. J. Ryan and J. Husslein (The MacMillan Company, 1920). For understanding the Aristotelian-Thomistic groundwork that led to the great encyclicals, tremendous work has been done by Rupert Ederer in a series of modern translations and commentaries. In particular, one should be aware of *The Social Teachings of Wilhelm von Ketteler, Bishop of Mainz (1811-1877)* (University of America Press, 1981); Heinrich Pesch, *Liberalism, Socialism, and Christian Order*, 4 vols. (Mellen Press, 2000); and *Teaching Guide to Economics*, 4 vols. (Mellen Press, 2002).

About IHS Press

IHS Press believes that the key to the restoration of Catholic Society is the recovery and the implementation of the wisdom our Fathers in the Faith possessed so fully less than a century ago. At a time when numerous ideologies were competing for supremacy, these men articulated, with precision and vigor, and *without* apology or compromise, the only genuine alternative to the then- (and still-) prevailing currents of thought: value-free and yet bureaucratic "progressivism" on the one hand, and the rehashed, *laissez-faire* free-for-all of "conservatism" on the other. That alternative is the Social Teaching of the Catholic Church.

Catholic Social Teaching offers the solutions to the political, economic, and social problems that plague modern society; problems that stem from the false principles of the Reformation, Renaissance, and Revolution, and which are exacerbated by the industrialization and the secularization of society that has continued for several centuries. Defending, explaining, and applying this Teaching was the business of the great Social Catholics of last century. Unfortunately, much of their work is today both unknown and unavailable.

Thus, IHS Press was founded in September of 2001 A.D. as the only publisher dedicated exclusively to the Social Teaching of the Church, helping Catholics of the third millennium pick up where those of last century left off. IHS Press is committed to recovering, and *helping others to rediscover,* the valuable works of the Catholic economists, historians, and social critics. To that end, IHS Press is in the business of issuing critical editions of works on society, politics, and economics by writers, thinkers, and men of action such as Hilaire Belloc, Gilbert Chesterton, Arthur Penty, Fr. Vincent McNabb, Fr. Denis Fahey, Jean Ousset, Amintore Fanfani, George O'Brien, and others, making the wisdom they contain available to the current generation.

It is the aim of IHS Press to issue these vitally important works in high-quality volumes and at reasonable prices, to enable the widest possible audience to acquire, enjoy, and benefit from them. Such an undertaking cannot be maintained without the support of generous benefactors. With that in mind, IHS Press was constituted as a not-for-profit corporation which is exempt from federal tax according to Section 501(c)(3) of the United States Internal Revenue Code. Donations to IHS Press are, therefore, tax deductible, and are especially welcome to support its continued operation, and to help it with the publication of new titles and the more widespread dissemination of those already in print.

For more information, contact us at:

222 W. 21st St., Suite F–122~Norfolk, VA 23517~(757) 423–0324
info@ihspress.com   www.ihspress.com   fax: (419) 715–0361

IHS Press is a tax-exempt 501(c)(3) corporation; EIN: 54-2057581.
Applicable documentation is available upon request.